GETTING PROMOTED

OTHER BOOKS BY HARRY E. CHAMBERS

The Bad Attitude Survival Guide: Essential Tools for Managers

No Fear Management: Rebuilding Trust, Performance and Commitment in the New American Workplace, co-authored by Dr. Robert Craft

GETTING PROMOTED

Real Strategies for
Advancing Your Career

HARRY E. CHAMBERS

PERSEUS BOOKS
Reading, Massachusetts

ISBN 0-7382-0102-2

Library of Congress Catalog Card Number: 98-83276

Perseus Books is a member of the Perseus Books Group

Cover design by Bruce W. Bond
Text design by Faith Hague
Set in 10-point Stone Serif by Faith Hague

123456789—0302010099
First printing, March, 1999

Perseus Books are available at special discounts for bulk purchases in the U.S. by corporations, institutions, and other organizations. For more information, please contact the Special Markets Department at Harper-Collins Publishers, 10 East 53rd Street, New York, NY 10022, or call 212-207-7528.

Find us on the World Wide Web at
http://www.aw.com/gb/

As always,
To Chris, Patrick, Shari, and Michael

*To my sister, Pat Hess, whose fierce love and devotion willed our father
to recovery. She and her husband, Bob, have gifted him with additional
years of celebrated life through their loving, nurturing care.*

CONTENTS

ACKNOWLEDGMENTS

This book blends years of personal experience in the workplace with input from many exceptional people who were open to sharing their thoughts, ideas, and experiences. Heartfelt thanks go out to my family—my wife Chris, and son Patrick—for their support and willingness to sacrifice during the creation of this book. Chris also played an important role with her editing, motivational, and problem-solving skills. She was truly a partner in this endeavor.

Once again, my assistant, Mickey Beatty, made a major contribution in preparing this manuscript for publication. Her flexibility and hard work are greatly appreciated. She managed to keep things moving even while welcoming her first grandchild, Marie, to the Beatty family. Mickey is one of the "great" ones.

I am grateful to the very competent triumvirate at Perseus Books: Executive Editor Nick Philipson, who provided opportunity; Editor and Project Manager Extraordinaire, Julie Stillman, who contributed extremely valuable guidance, insights, and commitment; and Publicist Sharon Rice whose creativity and dedication make working with her an absolute joy.

A very special thank-you to all those who made specific contributions to this book. Some provided background information and others offered invaluable insight that was actually incorporated into the manuscript. Due to editorial decisions not all appear in print, and any cuts were based on space considerations, certainly not the lack of content quality. All made valuable contributions: trainer, author, and public speaker, Lani Arredondo; David Haddock, Joe Dawson, and Scott Cutting from Pratt and Whitney Aircraft; Art Lucas, President of The Lucas Group; Priscilla Hall, Alcon Laboratories; Oliver Jordan, Pennsylvania Convention Center; David Tate, East Manufacturing Company; Barbara Mauntler, Sun Oil Co.; Frank Condello, Nebraska Book Company; and Charles J. Lathram with Bell South. Countless others also shared their thoughts, frustrations, and strategies on being promoted.

INTRODUCTION

Randy worked for an organization in the information service industry for a number of years. He was a loyal and productive employee, had enjoyed consistent increases in his compensation over the years, and received reasonable acknowledgment of his achievements through formal recognition programs. The organization downsized once and had gone through a merger. The avalanche of change became more than he could bear and he decided to actively seek a new job. He engaged the services of a professional search organization and was actively interviewing with several companies in his quest for new opportunities.

In discussing his plans and activities with a close friend and mentor, some penetrating questions and comments surfaced. His friend commented,

Randy, you are leaving your current job because of all of the changes that are happening, and that's really interesting because you will actually become part of the change wherever you go. In your new job you will either be the driver of change or certainly an important spoke in the wheel of new ideas and activities. Organizations do not hire from the outside to maintain their status quo. You will be new. You will be the exception to the current norms. How will you respond to those people at your new company who are resistant to the change that you represent? You will probably find yourself exhorting them to view change as good, necessary, and in their best interests. You will be urging them to support the change because it's the future and it's important to be a part of the direction the organization is taking. You may judge harshly in others the same resistant behaviors you are already accepting and justifying in yourself. Maybe changing jobs is the right thing for you, or maybe not. However, it may be in your best interest to stay in your current job and dedicate yourself to growing your career rather than starting over somewhere else. While you may see opportunity in a new organization, your goals may actually be more readily achieved right where you are. If you just changed your perspective and intensified your efforts, you might be able to achieve significant promotion and career growth. The grass isn't always greener, and success frequently comes from plowing familiar fertile fields.

This book is for those who choose to seek growth, development, and promotability in their current jobs. Job change is always an option, but leaving prematurely or without taking advantage of every possible internal opportunity may close doors that will usually remain closed. Opportunity once lost can rarely be reclaimed. There is no statute of limitations on seeking new opportunities; however, you have invested a significant amount of time, effort, blood, sweat, and tears in your current job with your current organization. If you want to take the best advantage of your hard labor and service by moving upward in your career, this book will provide real-world strategies to help you in your quest.

This book was written to fill a huge void in available career-planning and strategizing resources. There is scant information available today to guide you through your pursuit of a promotion. Recent publications on career management strategies primarily focus on:

- Successful career changes
- Life's "second half" careers
- Interviewing for new jobs
- Dealing with downsizing
- Making what you "love to do" your actual job

Current resources ignore the question of how to make the best out of your present job. You have worked hard. How can you use that to your advantage and *not* have to start over elsewhere or "pay your dues" over and over again? This book focuses on enhancing your present position and reaping the harvest from the field you have already cultivated, planted, and nurtured. It may actually be detrimental to your career to abandon your current efforts and achievements just to start anew!

> ### *The grass is pretty green where you already graze.*

Contrary to popular belief, not everyone is changing jobs in today's economic environment. Let's shift the focus from changing to attaining maximum success in the job you have now. If you have "survived" the downsizing, already made the switch to a new job, or are ready to make that next move upward, this book is for you. Whether it's your first, next, or final promotion, this information will help you to maximize your productivity, creativity, and motivation to reach whatever heights your willingness, ability, and competence will allow.

You will learn:

- ◆ To confront today's promotion realities and identify how the challenges of the workplace have changed dramatically.
- ◆ The current critical skills that will get you promoted. (Yesterday's skills won't get you tomorrow's job.)
- ◆ The strategies and behaviors that are necessary to increase your promotion visibility.
- ◆ Performance appraisal strategies for utilizing the assessment process to your greatest personal advantage.
- ◆ What real-world managers are looking for in the internal people they promote.
- ◆ What makes organizations hire from the outside rather than promote from within.
- ◆ How to position yourself for the next promotion even if you have been denied the most recent opportunity.
- ◆ The career killers. (While these won't necessarily get you fired, they will get you "buried." Many people unintentionally "plateau" their careers without realizing it.)

Throughout this book you will learn from promotion mentors: men and women who have been promoted successfully and are currently promotion decision makers and influencers. Their experiences, thoughts, and action-based recommendations will help you design your personalized strategy.

Critical points of information will be presented as promotion navigational guides, which contain observations and specific action steps for mapping your success. They are highlighted by this symbol:

You will also find periodic assessments to help you determine your current level of skills, abilities, productivity or performance, and identify opportunities for growth and development. The value of these assessments increases proportionately with the candidness of your personal evaluation. If you rate yourself exceptional in every way, you deny yourself the vision of growth. We all have strengths and weaknesses. Be willing to honestly acknowledge yours.

This isn't theory—this is real-world application. It is your career. Are you willing to take responsibility for your own growth, development, and promotability? I sure hope so—because no one else is going to shoulder that responsibility for you.

Some perceive that promotions are based on luck. If so, we will help you to create your own good fortune! Being in the right place at the right time is an art, not a science. We will help you to be anticipatory about the places where you need to pitch your tent.

Bear Bryant, the legendary football coach at the University of Alabama, reportedly once offered this poignant definition of luck: "Luck is when preparation meets opportunity." You cannot control all aspects of the promotable opportunities within your organization, however, you do have total control over your own preparation. Your career is a journey. Prepare yourself to travel first class!

This book is not about working harder—you are already doing that. This book is about positioning yourself to be more "visibly efficient" and to be recognized as a critical contributor to future organizational greatness. Somebody is going to be heading to the top. Why shouldn't it be you?

THE PATHWAYS TO PROMOTION

T he Point in Pittsburgh, Pennsylvania, is a landmark identifying the exact location where three separate rivers converge to form the mighty Ohio River, a much larger and more powerful waterway. This provides an excellent visual analogy of your quest to successfully achieve promotions and personal career growth. On your mission of promotability, three pathways must converge to create success, as indicated in the following illustration.

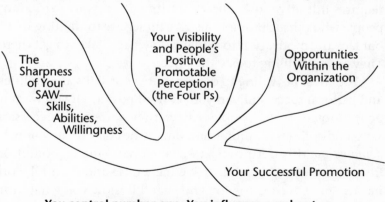

**You control number one. You influence number two.
You assess number three.**

Your Skills, Abilities, and Willingness

In his book, *The 7 Habits of Highly Successful People*, Dr. Stephen R. Covey identifies "sharpening the saw" as the seventh habit.[1] To be promoted successfully, you must continually sharpen your SAW.

- ◆ **S**kills
- ◆ **A**bilities
- ◆ **W**illingness

You must develop the skills and abilities not only to insure success in your current job, but also to enable you to be successful in the next job you seek. The skills and abilities that brought you where you are today are not necessarily the skills and abilities that will define success when you are promoted. Promotions frequently require the ability to work interactively and to get things accomplished with and through other people. This may call upon a whole new inventory of skills that you may or may not possess. Throughout this book, we will identify the skills and abilities necessary for success and assess your current personal strengths, weaknesses, and promotability. You will be invited to create a personal action plan to acquire any necessary additional skills, and to increase your visibility. However, this requires initiative, risk, and commitment on your part. Many people who pursue promotions give lip service to wanting them, but lack the motivation to actually do what it takes to get there. They are not willing to pay the price.

You must be willing to demonstrate your skills and abilities, and perform successfully in your current position if you want to be promoted. Many people believe they *possess* the necessary skills and abilities for promotion but are hesitant or unwilling to *demonstrate* this until they are given a permanent promotion first. Those who proclaim, "Give me a raise and then I'll work harder" or "Give me the job and then I'll show you what I can do," display a counterproductive arrogance that expects the organization to perform before they do! They expect the payoff before the effort and achievement. (Achievement and effort always come before payoff, even in the dictionary!)

Your Visibility and the Four Ps (People's Positive Promotable Perception)

There may be one or two people in the organization who will actually make the decision to promote you. However, there are many other "influencers" who impact the ultimate decision. Both decision makers and influencers must be made aware of your skills, abilities, and willingness, and perceive you as being promotable.

Your promotion success will be determined by how others perceive you.

Your perception of your skills, abilities, and willingness isn't enough; that same perception must exist in the minds of those who will be making or influencing the final decision. You do not have to like this fact, but you must accept it as truth. The perceptions of others may carry more influence than reality. Cultivating your visibility and image is critical to your future success.

Throughout this book, you will discover effective strategies for influencing the perceptions of others. Once again, this will take a significant commitment on your part. Are you motivated to do what is necessary to achieve your goal? The following assessment may be helpful:

Identifying Your Promotability Quotient (PQ)

On a scale of 1 to 10 (1 = never; 10 = always), complete the following assessment.

I consistently outperform my peers. _____

I work effectively in a collaborative or team environment. _____

I take pride in my work (not displaying an "it doesn't matter" style). _____

I work well independently without constant supervision. _____

I rarely experience consistent or recurring personality conflicts with others. _____

I successfully resolve workplace conflicts. _____

I consistently communicate in a clear concise manner. _____

I consistently meet deadlines. _____

Tasks and projects move quickly through my area (I am not a bottleneck to others' achievements). _____

I take responsibility for problems (not blaming or shifting the responsibility to others). _____

I use good judgment and common sense in decision making. _____

I comply with policies and use organizational resources appropriately (never utilizing equipment for personal projects, etc.). _____

I do not allow personal problems or issues to interfere with my workplace behavior or productivity. _____

I resist feeding the rumor mill. _____

I refuse to talk about others when they are not present to defend themselves. _____

I extend appropriate recognition to others. _____

I listen appropriately and effectively. _____

I avoid expressing contempt or disregard for the organization, leadership, customers/clients, or coworkers. _____

I am internally self-motivated (not requiring others to motivate me). _____

I receive from others the exact results, information, or performance I expect from them. _____

Scoring:

180 and above: You are either very generous in your self-appraisal or you should already be running the organization! A second, third, or fourth opinion may be helpful to you in realistically assessing your skills. Key questions: If you perceive your skills, abilities and willingness to be so high . . . why don't others? Why haven't you already been promoted? It may indicate a lack of realistic organizational opportunity or inability to influence people's positive promotable perception of you. Rating yourself unrealistically may create a self-perceived lack of need for growth and development. This could be deadly in your quest for promotion.

160–179: Your promotion is probably on the horizon (if the organizational opportunity truly exists). Use this book to identify three key opportunities for:

- ◆ Specific skill and ability, growth and development
- ◆ Circumstances to demonstrate your extremely high willingness to succeed
- ◆ Influencing the perceptions of promotion decision makers and influencers

140–159: Congratulations on your honesty. This book will help you to identify the most important steps you must take to position yourself for a successful future promotion. Actively prioritize your challenges, concentrating on those you determine to be most important, and view your promotion as an intermediate goal—eighteen to thirty-six months.

Below 139: The good news is, there are lots of opportunities for improvement. Develop a plan to prioritize and pursue those opportunities. The realistic outlook is: promotion is not imminent—look long term.

Specific Skill Assessment

On a scale of 1 to 10 (1 = extremely low; 10 = extremely high), rate your specific knowledge and skills.

Your Current Job		The Position You Seek
_____	Technical job knowledge	_____
_____	Technical job skills	_____
_____	Overall industry knowledge	_____
_____	Verbal communication skills	_____
_____	Written communication skills	_____
_____	Listening skills	_____
_____	Organizational skills	_____
_____	Planning skills	_____
_____	Problem-solving skills	_____
_____	Conflict resolution skills	_____

Scoring:

A score of **8 or below** on any individual item indicates improvement opportunity. Rating every response **9 or above** probably indicates an inflated self-perception of skill and knowledge that may actually be interfering with your promotability.

Upon completing both of these assessments, provide a clean copy for your supervisor/leader and ask her to complete her assessment of you. Compare her assessment to yours. If the perceptions are relatively similar, you obviously have a realistic assessment of yourself. However, if there is a significant difference in any items on the two assessments, determine the root causes of the differing perceptions and identify what you can do to change them.

Success will result when you identify what you can do differently, commit to actually implementing the change, and make your supervisor aware of the specific transformation. Do not become defensive and tell her she is wrong. Seize the golden opportunity to look in the mirror. If possible, circulate this assessment to as many promotion decision makers and influencers as possible and ask them for their candid input. The more information you can gather concerning how others perceive you, the better you can determine the effectiveness and quality of your strategic decisions.

Influencing the Four Ps

In reality, people's positive promotable perception is something over which you may have no direct control; however you do exercise significant influence. To accomplish this, you have nine tools, or spheres of influence, which you can utilize to create or alter the perceptions of others. No one possesses 100 percent command of all nine of these influences. It is extremely important for you to analyze your personal strengths and weaknesses and commit to developing specific strategies to take full advantage of those that work for you, and improve, neutralize, or abandon those that do not.

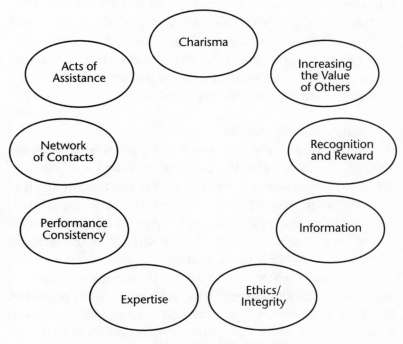

Changing the Perceptions of Others

Charisma

This is the art of being likeable and liked (the power of the personality). While some of us obviously have more personality than others, we all have some level of charisma. Learn to use yours to your advantage. Charisma can be positive or negative. If you walk into a room and everyone else clears out, you probably will not be promoted any time soon!

Charisma is frequently described as personal "chemistry" and has many components. Chief among these is the ability to put people at ease, to help them to enjoy themselves, and to make them feel that they are valued and important to you. Unfortunately, many people equate charisma with becoming the charming, silver-tongued, glib entertainer. In reality, charismatic success hinges on the ability to relate to others. It frequently means listening to them and helping them feel that they entertain you. Extending dignity and respect to all is extremely important. We tend to like and welcome those who treat us well. Having an abrasive nature may make you feel superior, but it won't enhance your promotability. People who are liked are more accessible, are sought after more frequently, and are able to capitalize on contacts and relationships.

Recognition and Reward

You increase your ability to influence others when you celebrate their success, extend recognition, and share rewards. Your ability and openness in rewarding others and helping them to gain or acquire recognition is a very powerful influencer. Working hard to include others in credit or payoffs for achievements and accomplishments increases the influence they are willing to extend to you. Why? Because what gets recognized and rewarded gets repeated. When people realize that interacting or collaborating with you results in their being acknowledged or rewarded, they are very anxious to repeat their involvement and look to you for guidance. How often do your peers and superiors hear positive acknowledgment of their contribution and quality of work?

Take a lesson from the Academy Award winners. Their first utterances are "thank you" to their producers, directors, costars, and so on. Are these acknowledgments always heartfelt? Maybe not, but it gets them more movie roles!

Consider this: Often people actively pursue promotion by outperforming their peers. While this overachievement is in their best interest, attempting to do so at the expense of others, or by making others look bad in the process, is counterproductive. Frankly, this was the traditional path to promotion in yesterday's workplace. Today such destructive, competitive behavior can harm your promotability. (It doesn't help much in the charisma department either!)

 Internal competition has given way to internal collaboration.

Expertise
Possessing extensive knowledge or being seen as an expert in specific areas has significant influence on the people around you. This may include expert knowledge of:

◆ The technical process
◆ A certain segment of an industry or market
◆ Policy, procedures, or regulatory issues
◆ An individual customer or client base
◆ Current research or industry developments

When you are perceived to possess this unique knowledge or understanding of a specific area, you are considered the "person to go to" whenever there is a problem to be solved or advice to be rendered. People will want to tap into your expertise and seek your guidance, and with this comes an increase in your influence. Their positive perception of you expands as they rely on you more and more. Keep in mind, the key word here is perception. While you may be perceived to have special expertise, it may be no more encompassing than anyone else's. However, perception *is* reality. To have influence over others you must enhance their perception of your expertise and knowledge and be willing to share it to everyone's advantage.

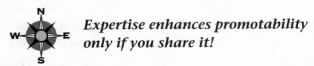

Expertise enhances promotability only if you share it!

Expertise not shared is expertise unknown and unrecognized. It does nothing to enhance your influence or promotability.

Information

Information is power. People who have information exercise significant influence over those who do not. They are believed to be "in-the-know" or "in-the-loop" and part of the "in-crowd." The more you know, the more influence you have. Typically information is doled out to some, withheld from others, and often becomes distorted as it cascades through many people, accompanied by the expected embellishments or inconsistencies. For information to provide an effective sphere of influence, it must be positive, factual, and shared appropriately. The influence of information does not include contributing to rumor, gossip, and the grapevine. While people are eager to hear juicy tidbits, they learn not to trust you because of your inability to keep confidences or your willingness to talk about others behind their backs. When your information is viewed as inaccurate, intentionally inflammatory, or self-serving, it severely reduces your influence. Others react negatively when information is used as a tool of manipulation.

Demonstrate a consistent willingness to share information equally with everyone and avoid, at all costs, creating the perception of playing favorites. Gather as much information as you can. Share as much as possible with everyone on an equal basis and learn to remain silent when necessary. Never exceed your authority in the dissemination of information.

Ethics and Integrity

While it is impossible to overstate the influence of ethics and integrity, it is also difficult to realistically define these traits in today's workplace. Situational ethics have become rampant and we are quick to accept and rationalize in ourselves behavior we deem unethical in others. Interpretation of ethics and integrity tends to lie in the eye of the beholder, though there are some meaningful guidelines.

During a discussion of honesty and integrity, a karate instructor was asked for a definition by one of his young students. The student asked, "I understand what honesty is. Always telling the truth and never telling a lie. But I don't know what integrity is. Can you explain it to me?" After pausing to think, the karate instructor responded, "Integrity is doing your push-ups when nobody is looking. Doing them because it's the right thing, not just because someone is watching you."

These sagacious words certainly help to define the consistency of ethics and integrity that will get you promoted. Refusing to take shortcuts, not sacrificing quality for expediency, being unwilling to do only what is necessary to get by, working harder even when the boss is not around or watching, are all real-world demonstrations of high ethics and integrity.

 In today's workplace, violations of ethics and integrity are commonly computer- or technology-related.

Today, temptations not available in the past are the basis for emerging ethical violations. Violations of restricted areas, computer hacking, running a business from work, online shopping, or the use of organizational resources or equipment for personal gain is on the rise and receiving increased monitoring and observation. These violations can get you in trouble real fast.

Also, the internally competitive practice of making others look bad or achieving success at the expense of your peers is seen as unethical behavior. The workplace paradigm has shifted away from winning at all costs!

Performance Consistency

This sphere of influence is earned over a period of time and is the ongoing demonstration of consistent, predictable, long-term top performance. It is not earned by displaying long periods of mediocre productivity with occasional spikes of high achievement. Your influence over the people around you increases when they know you can be counted on to deliver. When their expectations are consistently met, their dependency on you increases and this reliability enhances your promotability. While this may contribute to being taken for granted, more importantly, it creates the belief that you are someone they would want to be in a foxhole with when the shooting starts!

Such influence is not gained with one short burst of success. It is cultivated over an extended period of time. Consistency in performance can never be contested or denied by others, and it is perhaps the most important and enduring sphere of influence.

Network of Contacts

Maintaining a large inventory of personal contacts within the organization, outside in the broader industry, and throughout your community, increases your ability to influence others. You can serve as a referral base, or as a means of introduction for others, to those perceived to be in a position to help or to exert authority. This is extremely helpful in exerting influence and increasing your promotability. A large inventory of contacts also allows you to open doors for yourself and others, and increases resources and information sources. Developing a network of contacts isn't easy. It takes commitment and dedication. It means becoming involved in extracurricular organizational activities and volunteering for things that are not a traditional part of your job description. This requires an investment of time and effort; however, it may ultimately be one of the most powerful spheres of influence at your command.

Acts of Assistance

Your willingness to assist others and act as a resource for them increases your influence. This means extending yourself without waiting to be asked or without a specific quid pro quo. When you observe someone experiencing a crisis or engulfed in a deadline, act as an ally, someone who is looking out for him and his best interests, offer your assistance or recommendations for problem solving. This assistance can be extended to everyone at all levels of the organization. Observing when your boss is on overload and offering to help can be very beneficial, especially if it's in an area of high stress or low interest. Making this type of behavior a pattern in the organization increases the influence you have to positively impact others' perceptions of you. You become known as someone willing to pitch in and do what it takes. Although there is no specific agreement that "I'll do this for you if you'll do that for me," being helpful allows you to stockpile some implied IOUs, which may come in handy when you are working on an important, highly visible task or project.

Increasing the Value of Others

Helping others to experience learning, growth, and development also increases your influence. People who can teach, regardless of the specific learning that takes place, are given a larger sphere of influence and are seen in a very positive light by those who benefit from this skill or witness it in others. Are people more valuable to themselves or the organization for having interacted with you on a task or project? Do people see you as a resource to be drawn from or as a drain on their energy? This increase of value includes your willingness to share what you have learned even in the face of frustration and failure. You allow them the opportunity to learn from your mistakes without having to subject themselves to the same negative experiences. To increase your visibility, influence, and promotability, help people to learn new skills and assist them in their ability to reason through problems and challenges. Become a well from which learning is drawn.

Assessment of Your Spheres of Influence

	Yes	No
1. Do others feel comfortable in your presence?	☐	☐
2. Do you present yourself as somewhat aloof or above the need to socialize or mix?	☐	☐
3. Do you share recognition and reward appropriately, helping others to perceive a benefit of successful interaction or collaboration with you?	☐	☐
4. Do others perceive you as willing to succeed at their expense and exploiting their efforts as a means to achieve what you want?	☐	☐
5. Are you seen as possessing specific knowledge or talent above that of your peers?	☐	☐
6. Do others see you as being unwilling to share your expertise, perhaps threatened by their success?	☐	☐
7. Are you considered to be "in the loop" of the information flow? Are you seen as someone who knows what's going on around here?	☐	☐
8. Do people seek you out to hear the latest rumor or grapevine topic?	☐	☐
9. Do you do your push-ups when nobody is looking?	☐	☐
10. Do you take inappropriate advantage of the organization's technical capability, behavioral policies (phone usage, breaks, absenteeism, tardiness, etc.)?	☐	☐

11. Have you maintained an exceptional performance level over an extended period of time? Are you perceived as someone who can be counted on regardless of excessive workload or level of stress? □ □

12. Do others avoid involving you, doubt your willingness to keep agreements, or ability to perform under pressure? □ □

13. Are you well known and accessible to others in the organization, including those in totally different areas or functions from yours? □ □

14. Do you perceive yourself to be an island unto yourself, with no need to develop diverse relationships? □ □

15. Do you see opportunities to help others (including your boss) when they are experiencing the high stress of overload? □ □

16. Do others see you as someone reluctant to help out or go beyond your current job description tasks and responsibilities? □ □

17. Do you attempt to raise the value of the people around you? □ □

18. Are you seen as unwilling to help others increase their knowledge and abilities? □ □

Scoring:

In the odd-numbered questions, positive responses (*yes*) indicate strengths. For the even-numbered questions, negative responses (*no*) indicate strengths.

Your action plan:

◆ Continue to develop your strengths, get even better, and do more of it.

◆ Analyze your responses that indicate weakness and implement an appropriate corrective action.

◆ If all of your odd responses were *yes* and all of your even responses were *no*, go immediately to the dictionary and look up the word *denial*.

Performance Appraisal Opportunities

An additional, very valuable resource in your quest to influence the Four Ps is your annual or regularly scheduled performance appraisal. In chapter 9 we will address effective performance appraisal strategies in depth. At this point, consider the following factors of your performance appraisal.

◆ It is a formal opportunity to assess the perceptions, not only of your immediate boss, but of the entire organization.
◆ It provides the opportunity for you to formally state your promotion goals and identify areas for personal growth and development.
◆ Analyzing the appraisal criteria can help you to better understand the overall organizational thought process and culture.
◆ Learning to participate effectively in a personal performance appraisal allows you to position yourself above the crowd.

Your performance appraisal is much more than just an opportunity to seek a bigger raise.

Opportunities Within the Organization

In reality, you may possess all the skills, abilities, and willingness in the world, and everyone around you can be totally aware of your capabilities, but you will not successfully achieve a promotion unless legitimate opportunities exist within your organization. If all those above you are younger or members of the family, and there appears to be little or no growth or expansion of the organization in sight, guess what? You are not going to be promoted. You may be nominated for employee-of-the-century, but it still won't get you promoted. Obviously, you cannot be promoted unless there is someplace for you to go!

It is in your best interest to constantly reassess the realistic level of opportunity for promotion within your organization. Some things to consider in your assessment are:

- Is there an increase or decrease in your workload and others around you? What does this mean? Does it indicate growth or attempts to reduce the number of employees by reassigning their tasks?
- Are policies, procedures, and official communications directed toward growth or reduction (eliminating overtime, reducing travel, permanent elimination of expenses, etc.)? There is a distinction between prudent, thoughtful, profit-enhancing measures and extreme, reactive, radical measures that may indicate a current crisis or anticipated future problems.
- Is the organization financially equipped to pursue long-term growth?
- Would the current physical plant and infrastructure of the organization support significant growth? (Is expansion realistically possible?)
- Is the focus of the organization targeted toward today, or is it also looking toward tomorrow's growth and development?
- Is there a change in the observable behavior of individuals or teams above you, indicating their jobs may be at risk or the organization is suffering reversals?
- Do you find yourself having more or less access to the people above you?
- Are your creativity and input sought in significant decision making or problem solving?
- Are you being considered or passed over for important, highly visible, short-term projects or assignments?

- How many others have been promoted in the last three years? How do you compare in background, performance, and expertise?
- Does the organization attract or employ leaders oriented toward growth and capable of significant advancement?
- Is the organization positioned to be technically competitive in the next five to ten years of the current economic cycle?
- Are there other internal competitors for the same promotion you are seeking, who appear to be more highly favored?
- Have you or your department/team become farther removed from the core activities of the organization due to downsizing, restructuring, and so on?
- Do you have an antagonistic relationship with your supervisor/leader or any other significant people in the organization?
- Have you previously been passed over for promotion without explanation? Do you have a clear understanding of the adjustments necessary to insure success at the next promotion opportunity?
- Does your instinct or "gut hunch" tell you this organization is moving forward, just maintaining the status quo, or moving backward?
- What is the outlook for the industry? Is it growing, maturing, or sliding toward obsolescence?

An effective strategy for assessing realistic organizational opportunities is to seek the counsel of veteran employees. Talk to those who have been there for an extended period of time. What is their outlook? Most will be willing to share their thoughts and to help you make your determinations. Obviously, the introduction of any discussion must be framed in an extremely positive manner that in no way implies you are considering leaving or have any doubt or concern about organizational stability. It may be appropriate to start the conversation by saying, "I am really anxious to continue my career here and to seek as much growth and development as possible. What would you recommend that I do? What are the areas of greatest opportunity for the next five to ten years? How do you view the long-term outlook for the organization? If you were in my shoes, what would you do to get ahead?" Always be aware of personal agendas that may be articulated, and use any information you receive as a piece of the overall picture. Be conscious of the potential for the pump up and the poison. Some may perceive it's in their best interest to paint a rosy picture, others may wish to use the opportunity to vent years of past resentment. Your objective is to discover other people's perspectives and carefully evaluate the input they may offer. Seeking the wisdom of others, and perhaps inviting a mentoring relationship, can be valuable in developing an objective opportunity assessment and helping to formulate your strategies for promotion.

 Clearly assess the realistic potential for successful promotion.

Do not spend irreplaceable effort and time in pursuing opportunities that have a low probability of materializing.

In the next chapter, we will look at the specific promotion realities of today's workplace. This will begin to establish the ground rules and further identify how today's promotion challenge is far greater and different than at any time in our economic past.

TWO

TODAY'S PROMOTION REALITIES (TPR)

Achieving promotion, rising to the top, and moving up the corporate ladder have never been as difficult and challenging as they are today. In the past, the path to promotion was relatively clear and well defined by tradition. Today's promotion is met with previously unknown obstacles and traps. The rule book has been rewritten.

In the past, promotions were predictable. You could expect a minimum of two or three upward moves in your career as you invested twenty-five or thirty years with the same company. Promotions were frequently based on longevity or internal politics, and those who lived and breathed the longest were traditionally rewarded with promotions. You moved up in the organization by outlasting your peers. In the past, many people were promoted because they "deserved it," and organizations frequently created positions to "pay people off" because it was expected and it was the right thing to do. Those quaint times of yesteryear are long gone. They are chapters in the economic history book and reflect the good old days which aren't here anymore, and no matter how good they may have been, aren't coming back!

In this era of streamlined organizations:

♦ There are fewer upper-level jobs to be promoted into.

♦ The competition for promotion opportunities has never been as fierce or intense.

♦ Even organizations experiencing explosive growth are creating proportionately fewer upper-level positions.

♦ Today's "do more with less" world demands increases in responsibilities and accountabilities, frequently without additional compensation or acknowledgment of promotion. (You're doing the job but don't have the title or paycheck.)

Today's promotability is defined by productivity as the influence of longevity decreases. Birthday cakes, cards, and presents are today's payoff for doing your job another year. Those moving up are those who are most productive. Longevity and productivity frequently exist in the same person; however, when they do not, productivity is beginning to carry the day. Internal politics still remain (and always will!) a powerful determining factor in promotion decisions. Today's political advantages are gained by being effective, productive, and demonstrating high achievement, not by the traditional way of "sucking up," brownnosing, and kissing anatomy!!

This chapter describes some of the most significant promotional facts of life in today's workplace. Whether you like them or not, find them fair or unfair, right or wrong, reasonable or unreasonable, frankly doesn't matter. If you want to successfully win the competition for career growth, you had better learn the rules of the game, and these realities provide the foundation for today's rewritten promotion rule book.

TPR #1: You Will Not Be Promoted Because You Deserve It— You Are Not "Entitled" to Anything

Okay . . . so you think you *deserve* to be promoted. Well, guess what? Everyone else thinks they deserve to be promoted too! Of course, you *are* a wonderful, dedicated, hard-working, committed employee (in your eyes), but get over it, because this is *not* a basis for promotion. It could be that you and your mother are the only people on Planet Earth who share that perception!

No one is going to create a promotion for you in today's economic environment just because you think you deserve it. Promotions must be earned and paid for with the hard currency of visible achievement. When we believe our self-perceived past accomplishments are enough, we lull ourselves into thinking we have paid our dues and have a right to slow down until the rewards begin to materialize. This frequently degenerates into resentment and negativity, perhaps escalating to seething bitterness when the deserved promotion doesn't materialize fast enough to meet our expectations. Resentment, negativity, and bitterness are not traits that tend to contribute to promotability. The negative impact is compounded by acting out or vocalizing these frustrations. How many times have you heard people proclaim, "I've been killing myself around here for years and I never get promoted. Why should I keep doing this?" Or, "When I get promoted I'll work harder, but not until then." This self-righteous indignation is usually seen by others, including promotion decision makers and influencers, as whining and complaining.

Yes . . . in the past, positions were created for people because they were hard-working, loyal, devoted employees who were entitled to be rewarded and deserved to be promoted. They were promoted to keep them happy and to serve as a visible example to all employees of the company's willingness to show appreciation to their hard-working people. Frequently these created positions were peripheral and not critical to the core mission of the organization. These positions contributed to organizational bloating, and when the eventual feeding frenzy of downsizing occurred, these nonessential, low-contributing positions were purged. As organizational obesity ballooned, the crash diet of job elimination was triggered in part to regain some form of balance and control.

Do not allow yourself to fall into the trap of "I've already paid my dues" thinking. Dues are never paid in full. We all must campaign for reelection every day.

TPR #2: There Are Fewer Promotion Opportunities Available in Today's Flattened, Downsized, or Reorganized Companies

Traditional, middle-, and upper-level management positions are being reduced and the control of the average American manager is increasing dramatically. When existing positions do become available, the knee-jerk reaction to find a replacement as soon as possible is being replaced by the chorus of: "Is it necessary to refill this position at all?" "How can we maintain quality and productivity without filling this vacancy?" "Can we blend other's duties and eliminate this job altogether?"

These jobs are frequently eliminated by expanding the duties of existing personnel. The standard job description safety net of "other duties as assigned" has taken on a life of its own as we increase the responsibilities of existing people and avoid filling vacant slots. The jury is still out on the overall effectiveness of downsizing and reorganization. Assessment of the long-term repercussions of these strategies is still to be determined. However, the reality is, there are fewer jobs to be promoted into!

The good news is, advanced technical positions are expanding and creating new promotion opportunities, though those previously sought-after middle- and upper-level management positions are becoming fewer and fewer.

TPR #3: The Competition for Promotion Is More Intense than Ever Before in Our Economic History

As there are fewer jobs to be promoted into, more and more highly capable, competent and productive people are going to be competing for fewer opportunities. To win the competition, you are going to have to prove your exceptional performance capabilities, and consistently demonstrate a positive attitude exemplifying your determination to succeed. For every one promotion opportunity, the average organization has a minimum of four potential candidates for promotion. Being good isn't good enough; you have to be the best and possess the abilities to help the organization move forward.

TPR #4: The Life Span of "Potential" Is About Three Weeks!

In the past, promotions were given to people who were perceived as having great potential. Some people were able to ride this perception of potential for a long time; some retired still waiting for their potential to materialize! Not anymore. Potential has given way to the necessity of demonstrating current measurable performance.

 You do not gain promotion based on what you are going to do, you gain promotion by doing it.

If you seek the opportunity to lead a department, then prove it by successfully leading a team. If you want the opportunity to increase productivity on a large scale, prove your ability by increasing productivity in a smaller, visible, well-defined way. If you want the opportunity to improve the productivity of others, prove your ability to increase your own productivity and demonstrate specific examples of your positive impact on the performance of others. If you want to make things happen on a grand scale, begin to make them happen effectively in a smaller arena. The claims of future greatness ring increasingly hollow, while the proof of current achievement resonates with permanency. If you think promotion comes before contribution and performance, you have been reading too many fairy tales!

TPR #5: Promotability Is Enhanced by Increasing the Overall Value of Your Contribution

Increasingly promotions are determined by the value brought to the new position. Key question—"Will promoting you result in creating greater benefit for the organization? If so . . . how?" Answer these questions and communicate your answers effectively to the promotion decision makers and influencers and you will have accelerated your promotability!

People who are perceived to contribute greater value are the ones who are earning promotions. What have you created in the past and what can you "produce" or "reduce" in your next position? Have you produced increased revenue, increased profits, increased efficiency, or increased quality? Have you reduced costs, time, staffing, or hassles?

If you have achieved any of the above in a measurable way:

◆ Do the promotion decision makers and influencers know it?

◆ How can you broadcast your achievements to even more people throughout the organization?

◆ How can you present your current achievements as indicators of future success?

◆ How can you expand your contribution and increase the success of the organization?

◆ Can you develop new services, products, processes, or methodologies?

◆ Can you champion an acquisition?

◆ Can you identify and create a new revenue stream or new expanded marketing opportunities for the current core business?

You can increase your value and promotability by helping the organization to do things

- ◆ *Faster*
- ◆ *Cheaper*
- ◆ *Differently*

- ◆ *More efficiently*
- ◆ *With greater magnitude*
- ◆ *More profitably*

TPR #6: Promotions "Look Different" from Before

Traditionally, promotions evolved around the pursuit of an ever-increasing span of control. When you were promoted, you managed more people. The more people you managed, the bigger the budget you controlled. The bigger the budget you controlled, the higher your ranking within the organization. While this traditional promotion path still exists, today's promotions frequently have a much different appearance and may actually entail managing fewer people, not more; managing or leading a process, not people; increasing visibility, influence, and responsibility without a formal job title change.

Today's current effectiveness is often defined by how few people are needed to accomplish the tasks or complete the process, not by how many. Promotions may mean influencing fewer people who are working together in collaborative environments, such as clusters or teams, and having increased influence and control over "things" (product lines, technical development, projects, quality improvements, etc.). Current promotions typically involve increased influence and responsibility over ultimate outcomes, not necessarily over people. Titles or job descriptions of today's promotion opportunities may not include a management role. Avoid the negative temptation of judging the value of a promotion position only by how many people are managed or the actual title of the job. The true measure of value is the scope of total responsibility, opportunity for continued growth, and the long-term, positive impact on your career and earnings.

At the end of this chapter, you will see a promotion mentoring example of how promotions *look different* today than ever before.

TPR #7: Superheroes Need Not Apply

Attempting to position yourself as indispensable to the organization, and becoming the one person who can do it all, has lost its luster. Organizations have become painfully aware of the danger of allowing such power, control, and influence to be concentrated in one individual. While being capable of "doing it all" is certainly an asset, actually doing so can be a severe liability. Today, superheroes may actually become the bottlenecks. When everything must go through them or they are the only ones who can do specific, critical tasks, everyone else is extremely dependent upon them and their performance. Others must wait for the superheroes' completion of their part of the process before anyone or anything else can move forward. Thus superheroes become convenient targets for blame and criticism. Missed deadlines and poor quality are frequently attributed to them regardless of their actual level of responsibility. Others may feel they need to take shortcuts or compress timelines due to the slowdown or bottleneck created by the superhero, and this perception is widely communicated in a negative fashion to various promotion decision makers and influencers.

Possessing the desire and ability to do it all yourself may be personally rewarding, however, it may carry negative baggage around issues of control or perfectionism that are not assets to promotability. Hoarding tasks and responsibility is not an asset, it is a severe liability, and can be a ticket to accelerated burnout, obsolescence, and perceived obstructionism. Teaching others to perform competently, raising their contribution and value, demonstrating your willingness to give tasks and responsibility away, and increasing the skill and knowledge base of others, actually raise your value to the organization.

If you make yourself indispensable and irreplaceable, how can you ever be promoted?

Learn as much as you can about as many functions, tasks, and roles as possible, but do not insist upon doing them all yourself. Learn to give them away. Refusing to allow others to learn and expand their boundaries is considered weakness. Being the perceived bottleneck or control freak can be to your career what Kryptonite is to Superman!

TPR #8: Leadership Skills Are Essential

Leadership has been defined as the ability to influence people without having to resort to exercising raw power from a formal hierarchical position. When you are successfully promoted, you will be given some degree of formal power, along with increased authority and responsibility. However, to successfully attain these positions, you must first develop your informal leadership. Informal leadership is the ability to influence without having formal power or position. (Recall the discussion of the nine spheres of influence in chapter 1.) Such informal leadership must be earned: it is not given. It is not defined by position or job description. People give their leaders influence willingly, by choice, not through demand or compulsion. There are many leaders who are not managers and, unfortunately, there are many managers who are not leaders. It is not uncommon for informal workplace leaders to actually have more influence over their peers than those who may be in formal positions with impressive titles. Managers are ordained, given positions of authority, and manage activities within the existing policies, procedures, and boundaries of the organization. Management authority rests in the title of the job. When the title is taken away, the power erodes significantly. There are few individuals less influential than ex-managers! Leadership endures and cannot be taken away. Leadership can be forfeited, as when leaders violate the trust of the people around them. However, leadership endures while managerial influence is transitory.

The Four Agencies of Leadership

How is informal influence earned? By developing the four agencies of leadership. Individually, they positively impact your influence over others and increase the respect others have in you. Effectively blended together, these four agencies define workplace leadership.

Become an Agent of Preparation

Be an asset to others by preparing them to meet the challenges of the future. Equip them to meet the emerging opportunities of tomorrow. Key questions: Are employees better prepared and worth more to themselves, the organization, and the people around them because of their exposure to or relationship with you? Do you tear them down or build them up? Do you help them to get better or keep them down to minimize their potential threat or competition? These are tough questions. Go look in the mirror . . . are you looking at an agent of preparation?

Become an Agent of Options

Help the people around you to identify options and alternatives in the face of challenge or crisis. Expansion of options is critical to success in today's workplace. When people complain about their jobs, their bosses, and so on, rather than reinforce their complaints, help them to look at their options. What can they do to correct the problem or deal with it more effectively? If they are having trouble with a project or task, help them to become solution oriented. Reinforcing the status quo is not leadership, it is a perpetuation of current discomfort. It takes no talent to be a problem identifier by joining in and escalating the venting. It takes significant talent to be a problem solver, and the successful solution to problems begins with an examination of options. This is *not* telling people what to do and expecting them to be obedient, nor is it taking the responsibility for solving their problems for them. Becoming an agent of options is broadening their vision by helping people to identify possible alternatives and allowing them to select their most effective solution. Victims perceive they have no options or control, and many people elect victimization as the easy way out. Options and alternatives defeat helplessness and hopelessness.

Become an Agent of Closure

Leadership is future focused. Its antithesis is maintaining a consistent fixation on the past. Some people choose to continue to live in the negative issues of the past. They keep themselves "churned up" over past experiences of perceived unfairness, disrespect, callousness, or abuse. They frequently make past issues the focal point of their current conversations. Thoughts, actions, and even positive current events can somehow be linked to negative episodes of the past. To demonstrate your leadership skills, identify ways to help people bring closure to the issues of the past and move on. Listen to their issues . . . once . . . and then redirect them with phrases such as: "How can you get past this?" or "What will fix this for you?" or "What will help you to begin to look at what's ahead, where you're going, instead of where you have been?" Some of the past issues people cling to are legitimate, some are based in a perception of "poor me." Unfortunately though, none of the past can be erased. Acknowledge the past, learn from it, and move on.

 True leaders do not permit the past to dictate the present or hinder the future.

Become an Agent of Change

Change is inevitable. It is the one consistent factor confronting every organization today. Let's face it . . . if you are in an organization that is not confronting change, you are really in a funeral procession heading to the cemetery! If this is the case, you may want to drop out of line, accelerate past the slow-moving traffic, and head in a new direction.

Some are able to embrace change and move forward, while others who are intimidated or threatened by it, dedicate themselves to attempting to maintain the status quo. However, change is a freight train that will not be stopped by erecting barriers along the track. You do not have to welcome or agree with the change, but you must comply with the demands of change, or, frankly, seek other employment. Change is not easy, and workplace change, though chosen by a very few (owners, boards of directors, CEOs, etc.), is imposed or inflicted on the many. Those who can help others to successfully embrace change and break down their internal barriers are talented, valuable, and promotable.

Agents of change focus on two issues: communicating the vision, and communicating the consequences.

◆ **Communicating the vision.** You develop your role as an agent of change by continuing to paint the vision of the positive direction and intended outcome of the change. Consistently restate the ongoing mantra: "This is *why* we are changing. This is *where* we are going. This is *what* we are going to accomplish." If people are expected to endure the discomfort of change, they must know the reasoning behind it.

Many people perceive that change is negative and they are quick to personalize it. Somehow the change is intended to punish them personally or make them uncomfortable. Broaden their vision and help them to see that change is driven externally by market forces, not internally by whim. The external challenges to the organization are changing very rapidly and management has to respond by adjusting its goals, policies, procedures, and behaviors if it is going to maintain effectiveness and drive future accomplishments.

◆ **Communicating the consequences.** Identify the downside of refusing or failing in your efforts to change. For many organizations the consequence of failed change is the inability to survive. No organizations or individuals have to change if they are willing to accept the consequences of their resistance or failure. The consequences must be clearly articulated and confronted. The consequences of failed change may be:

- ◆ Obsolescence
- ◆ The inevitability of status quo maintenance
- ◆ Outsourcing of failed change initiatives
- ◆ Diminished influence, access, or power
- ◆ Downsizing or termination

The vision is the positive intent of the change initiative. The consequences are the negative outcomes caused by a failure to implement the change. Raise people's awareness of these two issues, continue to reinforce their importance, and lead by your own personal examples. Being an agent of change and developing the skills of leading people into tomorrow is a highly promotable skill.

TPR. #9: Interactive Team Behaviors and the Proven Ability to Work with Others Increase Promotability

"Doing more . . . with less . . . " in a collaborative effort is the anthem of today's organizations. Being the Lone Ranger, by defending your turf and becoming an impediment to collective achievement by refusing to support the efforts of others is a certain career death knell. Seek opportunities to demonstrate your eagerness and ability to achieve in an interactive team environment. Being able to tap collective creativity, intellects, and talents is a very promotable skill. The traditional "look at me, I'm great, look what I've done" self-promotion will *not* help successful career growth. (It won't make you real popular with your peers either!) Today's workplace demands:

- Developing a *we vs. me* mentality
- The ability to problem solve in an interactive team or group environment
- The acceptance of diversity in ideas, people, and styles
- Participative vs. competitive alignments
- Positive contributions and behaviors in meetings and discussions
- The skills to resolve group conflicts
- Clear, concise communication with others
- The willingness to accept positive criticism

TPR #10: Exceptional Technical Skills Are Necessary, but Are Not Enough

Unquestionably, technical proficiency is essential for success in today's work environment. It is the foundation of a successful career. If you don't have technical skills, you can't possibly be successful, however, skills alone will *not* get you promoted. They are the beginning, but not the end of your quest. To position yourself for upward acceleration, you must expand your skill base to include relationship (people) skills and organizational skills.

Relationship Skills

The ability to:

- Communicate effectively.
- Listen actively (the least practiced skill in today's workplace).
- Calm disgruntled coworkers and customers.
- Get along with others.
- Diagnose problems accurately.
- Solve problems creatively.
- Resolve conflicts fairly and productively.
- Develop and follow action plans to successful conclusions.

Organizational Skills

The ability to:

- ◆ Establish and maintain a clean, efficient, orderly desk or workspace!
- ◆ Structure your work (and the work of others) in a logical, productive, effective sequence.
- ◆ Manage the paper flow—some people are denied promotion because they do not know which pile to put their latest piece of paper on.
- ◆ Establish and maintain an orderly filing system.
- ◆ Develop an efficient daily plan.
- ◆ Demonstrate goal-setting skills: short-term, intermediate term (six to eighteen months), and long-term (greater than eighteen months).

 Your promotability is enhanced by how well you implement and showcase your interrelational and organizational skills.

Many people who have messy desks or disheveled workspaces truly believe these are their personalized, effective filing systems. "I know it looks messy, but I know where everything is." This is self-delusional, but even if it were true that the chaos was somehow efficient, the fact cannot be denied that the disorganized appearance sends a horrible message to others. It creates the indelible impression of total and disastrous *dis*-organization. It is a concrete indicator of the inability to deal with your current workload. "If they can't keep up with their current job, why would we promote them into something even more demanding?" Don't con yourself into thinking that everyone else has the same faith in your system that you do. Your *system* may paint an ugly picture, and the perceptions others draw are beyond your control to change or correct.

Consider this: Think of the people you have known throughout your career who you perceived to be the really great ones or the superstars. These men and women were truly the exceptional performers. (The people you would like to clone if you were starting your own organization.) What made them great? Was it their technical skills? Probably not . . . odds are it was their interrelational and organizational skills as well as their technical skills that truly defined their greatness. Yes, they were technically competent, however, it was their superior relational and organizational skills that actually set them apart.

In today's workplace technical competency makes you good enough to keep your job. The organizational and relational skills in addition to your technical competence make you great (and promotable!!!).

TPR #11: You Must Demonstrate Self-Educability

 You are responsible for your own greatness!

Unfortunately, in today's workplace, most organizations are not effectively training employees in all of the skills essential to success. It has been estimated that, at best, 50 percent of the necessary training is actually being offered: the other 50 percent is left untaught. Technical skill training is being provided, but the necessary interrelational and organizational training is not. This untrained 50 percent must be pursued on an individual basis or remain undeveloped. If you seek promotion, you cannot afford to rely solely on the limited training offered by your employer. Unfortunately, most people today are not taking the necessary initiatives to educate themselves, and they are content to blame the organization for the gaps in their training. While holding the organization responsible for this lack of training may be accurate, it is also convenient and self-serving. It results in skill deficiencies for which the individual pays an unacceptably high price. Do not fall into this trap. Face the reality and seize the opportunity to seek the additional training necessary to increase your inventory of skills. When you take the initiative, you gain a huge advantage over many of your internal competitors. This initiative involves taking a realistic self-assessment of your skill development needs, seeking input from your boss and other key people, and committing to an action plan of ongoing growth and learning.

Throughout this book you will find very specific recommendations on how you can pursue this necessary training and visibly demonstrate your willingness and dedication to improvement. Obviously, the traditional routes of formal college, university, or technical education are always available, and many of these institutions are tailoring their offerings to meet the needs of today's active, highly motivated, employed achievers. There is also a wealth of interrelational and organizational skill development publications on the market today. Skill development information is available on audio and videotape as well as CD-ROM formats. Interactive computer learning models are very effective. The opportunities are definitely there: it is up to you to take advantage of them. Do you have to take the initiative? No! It's okay . . . you can choose to sit back and watch others speed past you on the track to higher performance and promotion. Or you can actively seek additional growth and development in the areas that will impact your current performance and future promotability. It's up to you.

 You *are responsible for your inventory of skills: no one else will assume the responsibility.*

TPR #12: Establishing Trust Is a Cornerstone of Promotability

Similar to leadership, trust is first earned and then given. It cannot be coerced or demanded. It is also extremely fragile. Once violated or lost, it is difficult or perhaps impossible to recapture. There are many components of workplace trust. Foremost among them are:

Keep Agreements

Do not give your word unless you are willing and able to keep it. Others are depending upon you and their performance may hinge on your ability to deliver. Dependability and trust are intertwined. Good intentions are not good enough. Others do not care how busy you are or what crisis prevented you from following through. They care about you keeping your word. Do what you say you are going to do! Think of your own circumstances. You know which coworkers can be counted on to keep their word. You can also identify the people whose commitments are not always followed up on. Trust erodes when agreements are not kept.

Listen

Fewer behaviors build trust more deeply and effectively than actively listening to others and seriously processing their input. It is proof of how highly you value their thought processes and intellect. It sends a tremendously positive message when you are willing to listen and invest your time and energy in others. Listening does not imply agreement, but it does acknowledge a legitimate right to have a thought process or opinion, and be taken seriously. People trust those who listen. Most of us don't listen effectively: we just wait impatiently for our turn to talk.

The skills of active listening will be discussed extensively in chapter 4.

Maintain Confidentiality

People trust those who prove they can keep information confidential. As previously mentioned, your trustworthiness and dependability are destroyed by spreading rumors, gossip, feeding the grapevine, or divulging confidential information. If you misuse confidential information, it quickly stops flowing toward you. Your pipeline and access will be reduced or eliminated. Violations of confidentiality usually begin with "Don't tell anyone I told you this" or "I'm not supposed to share this with anyone, but I know I can trust you." Not only do you violate the trust of those who initially gave you the information, you prove to those you are sharing it with that you can't be trusted with their confidential information either! When people confide in you or share sensitive information, honor them and demonstrate your trustworthiness by maintaining confidentiality.

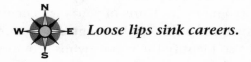 *Loose lips sink careers.*

Don't Take Credit for Others' Achievements or Ideas

Trust is destroyed quickly and effectively when someone takes personal credit for the good work or intellectual contribution of others. Taking credit for others' work may have limited short-term payoffs, however, there are huge, long-term, terribly expensive downsides to the loss of trust. If you have ever had someone else take credit for your ideas or productivity, you know firsthand how devastating and utterly complete this loss of trust can be. If your success is interwoven with others' ideas or efforts, be diligent in acknowledging and proclaiming their contributions. Trust, once lost in this manner, is rarely, if ever, regained.

Maintain Dignity and Respect

You do not have to like everyone with whom you work. Disagreements arise that may escalate into conflicts, but you should never treat anyone with a lack of respect or strip them of their dignity. Personal attacks, name calling, or talking about someone's "momma" are undignified displays that will cost you and your career dearly. Demonstrate your independent thought and be willing to challenge or disagree when appropriate, but only in a mature, dignified way. Challenge people's opinions and behaviors, but never attack their intellect or character. Common workplace violations of respect and dignity include:

- ◆ Talking about others behind their backs
- ◆ Subjecting people to emotional outbursts or public embarrassment
- ◆ Disregard for tact and consideration in communication
- ◆ Firing off heated memos or e-mails without considering the recipient's perspective and feelings
- ◆ Allowing the emotions of the moment to determine how someone is treated

It is difficult to trust and support people who treat you with disrespect.

Admit Mistakes

When you make mistakes, acknowledge them, learn from the experience, and move on. Attempts to project infallibility or refusing to admit when you are wrong will hinder your career growth. People who refuse to accept responsibility and blame others frequently find themselves isolated. Few people are willing to collaborate if they know they are just setting themselves up for blame. Demonstrate your ability to learn from your mistakes . . . don't hide from them.

People do not extend trust to those they must protect themselves from.

TPR #13: Contributing to Your Boss's Goal Achievement Increases Your Promotability

One of the most direct pathways to promotion is making your boss look good. This is one reality that hasn't changed over the years and never will! Help the boss move up the organizational ladder and you may get to take his place! Your boss has agendas: formal and informal, public and personal. Do you know what they are? Do you know what you can do to help him achieve his outcomes? Know what things are important to the boss, and accommodate his accomplishment in every legal, moral, and ethical way you can.

Whether you want to hitch your wagon to the boss's star, following him ever upwards through the organization, or be promoted into other areas of responsibility, having a track record of strong support of the people above you has an extremely positive impact on how others view your future.

Those who may become your boss in the future will be more welcoming of your candidacy for promotion if you bring with you a history of cooperating and contributing to your past bosses' successes and achievements. Let's face it—people tend to promote candidates they like —and nothing makes people like you more than helping them to look good!

TPR #14: Expenses Matter

Maintain a constant awareness of spending company dollars wisely. While you may or may not currently control the actual expenditure of dollars, your thought processes, recommendations, and actions should always demonstrate an awareness of judiciously watching the dollars. Making extravagant suggestions that involve significant spending can create the image of poor fiscal judgment. What opportunity do you have that will help you to demonstrate your financial wisdom? If you travel, you don't have to sleep in your car or have Tom Bodette keep the light on for you, but it is appropriate to incur expenses as if you were paying for them personally. It's all about perception. Don't spend $10 if $5 will do. Be aware of hidden costs.

- ◆ What does it actually cost the company to keep people tied up in a four-hour meeting when one hour would be sufficient?
- ◆ What does it really cost to add one more color to a printed brochure?

- What costs are incurred by hiring one new employee?
- Is it necessary to mail or ship everything for delivery the next business morning?

TPR #15: You Must Be Willing to Take Risks

If you sit back, play it safe, and wait for a promotion to come to you, you will probably do a lot of sitting and waiting. It is necessary to take appropriate risks that will accelerate your development and make you more visible to the promotion decision makers and influencers. Taking risks means showing initiative, making decisions or recommendations, and being responsible for creating outcomes. It is extremely important to prioritize potential risks and weigh their probable payoffs as well as their possible failures. The greater the risk, the greater the chance a positive outcome will dramatically impact your promotability, but also the greater the probability that failure will have a negative career impact.

Those unwilling to risk project an aura of uncertainty, reluctance, lack of confidence, perhaps low personal self-esteem, and an inability to take decisive action. Those who take risks present the appearance of a belief in their own competence and capability, and a willingness to learn from their mistakes. Key question: Is there a project to champion or a new initiative to launch that would demonstrate your willingness to take risks as well as your ability to follow the task through to completion? Appropriate risk takers, diligent in their selection and follow-through, are valuable organizational contributors who invite promotion.

People Who Get Promoted
- Are liked by others
- Avoid colossal failure
- Work harder when the boss isn't around
- Are good communicators (deliverers of the message)
- Listen effectively to comprehend the messages of others

- ◆ Demonstrate informal leadership before formal authority is attained
- ◆ Showcase their skills through effective reporting and documentation
- ◆ Positively confront conflict and disagreement—not choosing avoidance
- ◆ Look for ways to say yes, but say no effectively and assertively when necessary
- ◆ Seek to expand their influence and challenges by broadening the scope of their responsibilities
- ◆ Are successful at driving the process without losing sight of developing and nurturing people along the way

Real-World Promotion Mentoring

Promotions May Look Different from Before

Pratt and Whitney Aircraft, a division of United Technologies, has developed an internal program to focus on quality and process improvement initiatives. Planning for the program, which is known as ACE (Achieving Competitive Excellence), began in February of 1996 (under the direction of Louis Chénevert and designed by David Haddock, along with Joe Dawson and Rob Rourke). The driving force behind ACE was the statement:

Pratt and Whitney is committed to being the world leader in providing technologically advanced, dependable propulsion systems, parts, and services. We accomplish this by using the continuous improvement process to meet customer expectations, create employee opportunities, and achieve superior business results.

The mission statement of the ACE program is:

Achieve a level of quality and productivity improvement that will satisfy our customers and allow us to produce increased workloads more efficiently. This will be accomplished through the use of the tools of the Achieving Competitive Excellence process.

The Pratt and Whitney workplace is divided into business units referred to as cells. These are specific groups of machines and people, manufacturing a specific product, organized in a flow line manner, which is product focused. A typical cell consists of ten to twenty people. To drive the ACE program, employees referred to as Pilots have been selected for each cell, and they are responsible for leading their business unit through the growth and certification process. They face the challenges of raising awareness of the importance of the quality and process improvement goals, instilling support and motivation for change, and challenging the mindset of "how we've always done things around here." The Pilots are the actual implementers of the program. The typical background for Pilots is extensive experience in running machines, cutting chips, and manufacturing jet engine parts. They are working members of the various cells.

Officially, becoming a Pilot was not considered a formal promotion, though many found it to lead to even greater career opportunities. There was no compensation increase to entice people to move into the program leadership. Becoming a Pilot was an opportunity to break out of the repetitive past, move into something new to create meaningful change, and provide the background for individual growth into new and future career paths.

Joe Dawson, one of the original initiators of the ACE program, outlined the training and growth opportunity for the Pilots.

> *In one year they have over 200 hours of training on the seven major elements of the ACE process, plus other classroom, soft skills, and team facilitation training. They are very highly trained and are responsible for bringing these initiatives to their cell associates while working effectively with the cell leaders. They are responsible for orchestrating the whole ACE initiative within their specific cells. The skills and knowledge they are gaining now will be very useful in leadership positions in the future.*

The Pilots' training intense program includes:

- Communication skills
- Personal computer skills
- Organizational skills
- Presentation skills
- Software skills
- Interrelational skills

David Haddock stressed the importance of relational and collaborative team development skills.

> *In the ACE process, people know when they get into this leadership position, they are going to need the cooperation of everyone else in the cell. If they walk over everyone trying to get to the top, their leadership role is going to be very difficult. The change we have made at Pratt and Whitney through the ACE program requires total cooperation from everyone within the cell to make it effective.*

The ACE program has been extremely successful and was recently awarded the prestigious Arthur E. Smith Award (named in honor of a former CEO of United Technologies), one of the highest internal awards of honor and recognition within the United Technologies companies.

Becoming and effectively performing as an ACE Pilot may not have the appearance of a traditional promotion, however, it is an excellent example of the real-world growth and development opportunities in today's workplace.

THREE

FUTURE TRENDS AND CURRENT CHALLENGES

Future Trends

What will promotions look like in the future? What skills and abilities will be necessary for continued long-term success and ongoing promotability? If you knew the answers to these questions, you wouldn't need to worry too much about your career! You would have the greatest crystal ball in the world, and people would be knocking down your door for a perfect preview of the future. Obviously, no such thing exists, and while many legitimate futurists make their predictions of where the workplace is going, your best guide may well be your own intuition and common sense.

In chapter 1, we used the river analogy to emphasize the three factors that must converge to create successful promotability.

- ◆ The sharpness of your SAW (skills, ability, and willingness)
- ◆ The Four Ps (people's positive promotable perception)
- ◆ Opportunities within the organization

The illustration that follows demonstrates how this same analogy holds true concerning the future.

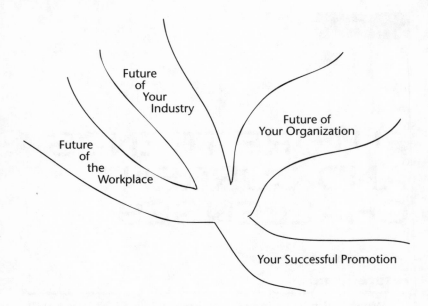

The Future Factors Impacting Your Promotability

The three tributaries or factors are: Where do you think the workplace is going? Where do you think your industry is going? Where do you think your organization is going?

There are obvious signs and trends that promise to influence the evolution of the workplace. While the intensity and contribution of each is yet to be determined, the reality of their impact cannot be denied. You will have to develop your own insight and evaluation of how they will affect your industry and organization.

The Reality of a Global Economy

We are no longer intertwined in local microeconomies or even one united national economic environment. Today and into tomorrow we are all competing in a global economy. In the past your competitors were local, perhaps located in the same community. You knew them well, and may have gotten together for lunch once in a while. Today your competitors may be halfway around the world and playing by a totally different set of rules. Patent and copyright protections and guarantees generally end at our borders. Some nations honor them, others do not. In many cases those who do not pose the greatest competitive threat.

In reality, the preeminence of America's global economic position is being challenged every day. The stability of the Chinese economy, the emergence of a unified Europe, and even the inconsistency of the Asian economies all pose significant competition to your nation, the market segment in which you are employed, your individual industry, and you personally. Key question: What can you do to position yourself to be more valuable and visible in this emerging global economy?

Consider this:

◆ **Command of foreign languages will obviously be of premium importance.** Traditionally, English has been the language of commerce throughout the world, but this is changing. The world is not necessarily beating a path to our door—we also have to go knock on theirs! Knowledge of Spanish, Japanese, Korean, and the Mandarin Chinese dialect will offer significant advantages to those able to communicate effectively in such languages.

◆ **Foreign culture and business awareness is an absolute necessity.** Familiarity with the law, business climate, prevailing customs, norms, and culture in key foreign markets will be extremely helpful. The "business of business" varies greatly from nation to nation and region to region.

◆ **Foreign banking and currency knowledge will be at a premium.** You won't have to be an expert, but a total lack of knowledge or familiarity may be a career stumbling block.

◆ **You must possess external global vision.** Possessing the flexibility and the ability to think strategically as well as to respond quickly, competitively, and effectively to external market forces is, and will continue to be, critical to long-term success and promotability. This includes the ability to identify significant changes and developments early in their cycles, allowing you to ride the crests of emerging waves rather than sucking water when the waves break over the top of you.

The Technology Explosion

The technology affecting your industry and your organization is being advanced, redefined, and recreated every day. To fall behind the technological curve is to invite obsolescence. Every industry and job function in America today continues to be subjected to ongoing technological redefinition and always will. Among the many challenges to you are the continual growth of your knowledge and the awareness of your industry's specific technological developments. Just being current in your knowledge isn't enough. You must stay abreast of what's coming next. There will also be many opportunities to utilize current technologies and developments in new circumstances. Key questions: How can you make better use of existing technology? Can you introduce it into other areas?

Maintaining your technological edge demands a commitment from you. Professional publications, industry or career-related associations and societies offer excellent opportunities and require an investment of time and effort on your part. It is also extremely important to develop and maintain a network of contacts related to your industry or job function.

The continuous questions that should be ever-present in your mind are: Where do you see technology heading? How do you think you will be doing technologically five to ten years from now? What's the next technological breakthrough?

The Information Age

The volume of information available today is beyond comprehension and becomes ever greater with each setting of the sun. The impact of today's gargantuan information flow is the dominant reality in the workplace. Your ability to use information technology effectively will impact your promotability.

Lacking these skills will insure failure or permanent relegation to lower or perhaps even remedial job classifications. You must keep your computer and information skills current and forward looking. You don't have to be the brightest rat in the maze, nor can you afford to be perceived as the dumbest!

There are three critical factors entwined in the challenge of today's escalating informational resources.

1. The ability to access and utilize the available information. You have to be able to get to it!
2. The ability to process large volumes of information. Information overload is real and it is worsening each day. You must develop personal and computer/technology-driven methods to accommodate the absorption and processing of huge volumes of information. (Technology and time are of paramount importance.)
3. The ability to determine which information is really important. Everything in the teeming flow of information appears to be of critical importance. It all looks the same. So, you have to have the ability to prioritize and discern what information is critical and useful from that which is interesting but not critical, or altogether meaningless.

Most of us are able to identify and eliminate meaningless information, however, the real battle must be fought in separating the interesting from the critical. You cannot afford to invest time and effort in absorbing and processing information that is merely interesting but not critical to your success or the organization's core mission.

Customer Service Capabilities

As we continue to cascade from a predominantly manufacturing-based to a service-oriented economy, the skills of customer service will prevail. The intensity of today's competitive economy and the wealth of options available to clients, customers, patients, students, and the like, demand that you be highly skilled at providing exceptional service to insure ongoing relationships with your customer base. The inability to do so results in the withering and dying off of organizations and industries. If you are the only game in town, customer service doesn't matter, people do not have a choice, but as soon as another game opens up—you're out of business! Even in the public sector, customer relationships are being redefined. Taxpayers are seen as customers (just ask the IRS!), and if they are not, they certainly should be. Government agencies that do not provide customer service experience funding challenges. Even traditionally noncompetitive entities are now under intense competitive pressure to provide exceptional service. The IRS and many state and local service departments (Department of Motor Vehicles, etc.) are becoming more taxpayer friendly. The dwindling of monopolistic or protected service environments demands that industries and organizations, which previously enjoyed locked-in customer bases, now compete. The ability and willingness to provide high-value customer service will gain importance as the future unfolds.

High-value, exceptional customer service is more than smiling and being nice. Though the importance of exceptional interpersonal skills should not be dismissed, it is becoming increasingly critical to:

◆ Identify current customer needs and expectations.
◆ Assess and continually upgrade the skills required to meet those needs and expectations.
◆ Train employees and staff in these skills.
◆ Constantly monitor and respond immediately to shifts in trends, needs, expectations, and customer demands.
◆ Continuously reevaluate your current processes, policies, and procedures to insure responsiveness.
◆ Introduce highly sophisticated monitoring and feedback mechanisms to evaluate your competitors' capabilities and innovations.

The Challenge of Continuous Learning

The shelf life of knowledge and ability is nanoseconds in today's workplace. What you know and do today may be obsolete and outdated tomorrow. The challenge of staying current is monumental and never-ending. The reality is, if you attempt to rest on your laurels or embrace the mindset that you've already paid your dues, you will be on the fast track to career exile. You must be willing to challenge yourself to continuously learn. You are in competition with yourself. Celebrate what you know, give yourself credit for what you have achieved, and constantly pursue the expansion of your knowledge and ability.

 Regardless of what the future holds, pursuing continuous learning is not optional, it is mandatory.

Any assessment of the future relies heavily on skill development in the following areas:

- Communication
- Organizational skills
- Problem solving/project management skills
- Interrelational skills
- Self-motivation/the ability to work in a nonstructured, self-directed environment

In chapters 4 through 8, we will identify real-world strategies for developing and showcasing these skills.

 A valuable tool for evaluating trends, challenges, and developing strategies, is to analyze the patterns of the people in your organization who have been successful in achieving promotion. What can you learn from them?

Current Challenges

There are many challenges to be met in attaining promotion, and some will be more easily surmountable than others. While everyone seeking promotion will experience challenges of varying intensity, and individual circumstances will generate unique responses, there are challenges that all hold in common and are predictable.

Insuring Others Expand Their Vision of You

How do others envision your current role? Capability and promotability are entirely different. You may be extremely capable in your current job, and everyone in the company may sing your praises, however, you must position yourself to be seen as capable of doing more. Throughout this book, we discuss the Four Ps (people's positive promotable perception of you) and offer strategies for enhancing their perceptions. This not only helps others to acknowledge your abilities and performance, it creates in them the vision of your advanced capabilities. It leads them to see what you could be tomorrow. If you cannot broaden their vision of your role, you may wind up in your company's Hall of Fame, but it will be for your current position. This is an extremely difficult challenge because others are in control of what they see as your role, and becoming permanently niched can be deadly to your career growth. You must be proactive and initiate additional activities or volunteer to do more than your current job requires. Don't wait to be asked, you may have to push the issue.

To wait is to:
__W__allow
__A__lways
__I__n
__T__oday

Avoid Being Pigeonholed or Placed in a Long-Term Assignment Out of the Mainstream

It is very difficult to maintain that high visibility and keep positive perceptions current when you may be in a less visible job or performing in an area that is not an integral part of the core mission or thrust of the organization. It is so easy to get lost. It is a fairly common occurrence for someone to be asked to serve for a short period of time in a nonmainstream job with the assurance from leadership that sounds something like, "Don't worry, this is only temporary, and we'll take care of you when it's over." While certainly well intended, these generalized, nonbinding commitments are frequently tossed to the wind and the placement becomes permanent. If you have any choice or influence in the matter, assess any short-term or nonmainstream assignment on the basis of overall long-term career impact. There is a scale to balance: on one side, not wanting to be seen as resistant or unwilling to support the good of the organization, counterbalanced by not wanting to put career growth on hold or risk what could become a permanent exile. If at all possible, negotiate these agreements in writing, clearly identifying duration of time and possible future options upon completion. It is not realistic to expect someone to promise you a promotion as a payoff for doing a particular job for a specific period of time, however, they certainly can identify the range of high-probability options that may be available.

If you are taking an assignment that is less visible, out of the mainstream, and off the traditional path to promotion, it is extremely important for you to have a crystal clear understanding of how your performance is going to be judged and what criteria for success or failure has been established. You can't win that part of the game if you don't know the rules. Clearly identify the goals and objectives of the temporary position, and understand how your boss and/or other promotion decision makers are going to view your performance. This allows you to tailor your activities and decisions specifically to the achievement of these predetermined criteria. Not only does this help to insure ultimate success, it also gives you the opportunity to maintain consistent visibility through targeted reporting with a wide pattern of distribution—when the goals and objectives are clearly identified, you can provide concise monthly reports to all concerned, trumpeting your progress and achievement.

 If the goals, objectives, and criteria are not clearly defined, your opportunities for visibility are severely hampered and you are basically playing in the dark!

Managing Potential Isolation

Telecommuting, working in a remote location, or being isolated from your boss and other promotion decision makers and influencers can present unique barriers to your promotability. Your lack of presence can be career damaging. Technological advances and the decentralization of many organizations have created circumstances where many people are working independently, from their homes, satellite offices, or away from the organization's central or home office location. This is a good news/bad news scenario. The good news is, the opportunity to demonstrate your self-motivation and ability to work effectively with little or no supervision certainly enhances your promotability. Also, not having your boss breathing down your neck is a welcome perk. The bad news is, the farther away you are from the mother ship (or the central location of influence), the harder it becomes to get promoted. The people closest to the epicenter of influence will have the advantage. If you are in a remote or detached circumstance, your communication skills will become extremely important. Communication will offer an opportunity as well as a potential trap. Your ability to communicate verbally and electronically will be critical in determining your promotion success, but poor communication skills can be deadly when working in remote circumstances. In chapter 4, we talk extensively about promotable communication skills, and this information should serve you very well.

As in the previously stated challenge, it is critical for you to clearly understand the goals and objectives of your job, along with (and perhaps most importantly) the expectations your boss and other promotion decision makers and influencers have regarding your performance. You may be in the hinterland, perceiving you are doing well, while they may be sitting back at home base judging you harshly.

Balancing Today's Productivity with Tomorrow's Growth

While your vision is focused on the growth of tomorrow, your feet and your efforts must be firmly planted in the soil of today. Doing both simultaneously is a significant challenge. The 80/20 rule can offer some guidance. Eighty percent of what you do should be clearly focused on the achievement of today's goals and objectives, meeting the current expectations of others, and the successful completion of your prescribed job duties. Twenty percent of what you do should be focused on preparing for tomorrow's challenges as well as assessing and communicating your vision of growth and change.

Being totally focused on today defines what you are currently. Broadening that focus to include a vision of tomorrow defines what you will become.

Influencing the Organization to Promote from Within

As a general rule, most organizations prefer to promote from within. There are significant advantages to doing so.

◆ Promotion candidates are "homegrown" and completely familiar with policies, procedures, and the organizational culture.

- Continuity creates a seamless continuation of the status quo.
- There are motivational benefits to providing a clear path of upward growth and mobility to productive employees.
- Cost is frequently a benefit. It is less expensive to provide an internal candidate compensation by way of an incremental raise than paying a higher price for external talent, not to mention the costs associated with hiring.

However, there are also disadvantages to promoting from within.

- Continuity creates a seamless continuation of the status quo (the way things have always done around here!).
- The available internal promotion talent may be marginal in the face of exceptional external candidates.
- Internal promotion candidates may bring widely known/ public, negative baggage. (This may include the "ugly warts" of inconsistency, past performance problems, disgruntled statements, or behaviors of resistance that are well known and vividly remembered by all. No matter how good recent performance has been, everyone recalls one's least flattering weakness.)
- When one successful candidate is chosen, there may be a wave of negative backlash from unsuccessful candidates. Internal jealousies and resentments may blossom as those candidates who weren't chosen typically perceive favoritism or discrimination of various sorts. Their responses may manifest as performance reductions and increases of negative, passive-aggressive, resistant behaviors that are all too common in today's workplace. Unsuccessful candidates frequently become leaders of the *un*loyal opposition and enlist others in their negative backlash against their successfully promoted peer.

How Can You Positively Impact the Decision to Promote from Within?

◆ Perform at such a high level of productivity that your candidacy cannot be denied. (This performance level must be in the eyes of your boss, promotion decision makers and influencers, not your eyes.)

◆ Keep yourself free of internal baggage. (Avoid performance inconsistencies, venting, resistant behaviors, and so forth.)

◆ If you are denied promotion, discover the specific reasons the decision did not go in your favor and work to overcome any perceived weaknesses. Position yourself to be successful at the next promotion opportunity. *Do not* demonstrate your disappointment through negative behaviors or performance that may bear long-term negative consequences.

◆ Position yourself as an agent of change, willing to support current policies and procedures, while enthusiastically embracing opportunities for change. Also, become a well-known source of reasonable and appropriate suggestions, strategies, and techniques to meet the demands of the future.

Regaining Momentum if You Were Passed Over for Previous Promotions

Given the intensity of today's internal competition for promotion, it's highly likely that you may be passed over for a promotion at least once in your quest to move ahead.

Losing is never easy. Be very careful that you don't self-destruct in the face of someone else's selection. Your emotional reaction and resulting behavior may well be under a microscope, and even in your extreme disappointment, you have a great opportunity to demonstrate your maturity and ability to deal with adverse circumstances. Do not fall into the trap of interpreting your lack of promotion as a signal from the organization that you're held in low regard. Sucking your thumb and pouting may be a normal and understandable reaction, but it will not enhance your career. If being passed over truly means that there will be *no* future promotions—and that was the one and only realistic organizational opportunity for successful growth—then factor this information into your long-term decision making. It may be in your best interest to move on, however, do *not* make an emotional decision that could adversely affect you, your family, and your career over the long haul.

Unsuccessful pursuit of promotion is a fact of life in today's workplace. Even such negative circumstances can be used to your promotion advantage.

Maintaining a Positive Focus in Today's Uncertain Workplace

It's very easy to fall prey to negativity and bad attitudes in today's workplace. The realities of flattened organizations, lack of employer/employee loyalty (in *both* directions), lack of job security, unfair compensation issues, being asked to do more with less, and many other circumstances collide to create a consistently escalating assault on anyone's positive perceptions. It is not easy to maintain a positive attitude, though when you do, you distance yourself from the crowd or the negative organizational herd. In my book, *The Bad Attitude Survival Guide: Essential Tools for Managers* (Perseus, 1998), I discuss the epidemic of bad attitudes and negativity in today's workplace. The book addresses the necessity for managers, or those who aspire to manage, to develop the skills for successfully dealing with oppositional attitudes or behaviors in themselves and others.

Don't give in to the negativity. While you don't have to like the changes and circumstances of today's workplace, you do have to live with them. You have two choices: you can learn to play today's game by today's rules and be successful and competitive (achieving the promotions and growth you want), or you can play today's game by yesterday's rules, with the only possible outcome being resentment and negativity (which creates a lack of growth and promotion). The choice is yours.

 It takes no talent to be negative.

Redefining Job Security

While many proclaim the death of job security, in reality this may not be the case. Job security has changed, but it is not dead. In fact, there may be more job security in today's workplace than ever before *if* you are willing to see it from a different perspective. In the past, job security was defined as the organization's responsibility to guarantee long-term employment to loyal and productive employees. As we all know, *that* job security no longer exists. Today's job security has become the guarantee of employability, not long-term employment. The responsibility for job security has shifted from the organization to the individual. Individuals guarantee their own job security by maintaining and enhancing their individual employability. You have more control over your job security today than ever before because the ultimate responsibility is in your hands.

 You guarantee your growth, security, and promotability by your own accomplishments and actions.

Meeting the Critical Credentialing Requirements

With fewer promotions to offer in today's streamlined organizations and the increasing competition among qualified candidates vying for those diminishing opportunities, organizations are becoming more and more selective in the requirements for promotion eligibility. Credentials count and may be considered a knockout factor, removing you from contention. Paramount among these are the formal educational requirements. In today's workplace you can work extremely hard, be very productive and effective in your current area of responsibility, and yet be denied promotion consideration because you do not possess the necessary educational credentials. It is incumbent upon you to know the educational requirements of the positions you seek and to meet those requirements. If you want to be promoted to a level that requires a specific degree or perhaps an MBA, and you do not currently meet that requirement or you are not *actively* pursuing its completion, frankly, you have an unrealistic expectation. Organizations are much more selective and are setting much higher standards for promotion candidates. Education, certification, licensing, and the like, *do* matter and have a huge impact on your promotability. Many organizations require either a completed degree or the active pursuit of such a degree to even consider you for a promotion. Demonstrating the willingness, not just the intention, can heavily influence circumstances in your favor.

Competition within and among educational institutions today has resulted in a wide array of options for those pursuing educational growth. Accelerated and external study programs, flexible hours, interactive team learning environments, and so on, all make educational development much more attainable today than ever before.

 If the degree, certification, or licensing is necessary, get off your anatomy and go get it!

Realigning, Reorganizing, and Restructuring

Mergers, buyouts, alliances, and so on, are constantly re-creating new organizational structures, ownership, and alliances. Opportunities are constantly being redefined, re-created, resurrected, and eliminated. The activity in the financial, telecommunications, transportation, and information systems industries alone are almost impossible to keep up with.

Today's competitor is tomorrow's collaborator. Today's predator is tomorrow's partner. While it's true that career growth can be abruptly altered by these activities, it is equally true that promotability can be enhanced, or perhaps rekindled, at an equal rate. Just as doors close, windows open. Keep in mind that while many people suffered during the horrible economic conditions of the Great Depression of the 1930s, others made money and created wealth under these same circumstances.

Do not permit yourself to see obstacles and roadblocks where others see opportunities.

The pervasiveness of today's climate of realignment intensifies the focus on your ability to stay currently abreast of technology, knowledge, and developments within your industry. Make sure you know what's going on!

Real-World Promotion Mentoring

Art Lucas is President, CEO, and founder of the Lucas Group, a professional staffing organization with regional offices in Atlanta, Dallas, Houston, Chicago, Phoenix, and Los Angeles. Among the divisions of the Lucas organization are:

◆ A military group with the largest service in the country for placing junior military officers after they leave the service

◆ A military technical division for placement of enlisted personnel possessing unique technical and communication skills

◆ An accounting/financial group recruiting CFO positions, staff accountants, and temporary contractors for the accounting/financial market

◆ A division specializing in executive searches for niche industries, among them consumer products, telecommunications, and plastics

The Challenge of Organizations Going to the Outside to Fill Promotion Positions

Art offered the following observations:

Organizations fill key positions from the outside for a number of reasons. First of all, they don't have the current talent inside to drive the business at the speed or rate they want to move it. That is probably the primary reason. They may have an internal need, either through a termination, expansion, or something happening to the person currently in the job, and they don't have the talent internally to promote. The second reason they go to the outside is they want to change dramatically. There may be a real need to change the direction of the business, and the people internally have been doing it one way, and that way probably isn't working anymore. Organizations find it a lot quicker to initiate change through bringing in change agents who have accomplished it somewhere else and who bring a track record. Someone once said to me, "You can hire better in fifteen minutes than you can change a workforce in a lifetime."

When asked what he looks for when promoting people within his organization, Art responded:

We obviously look for people who have a success pattern in their past. I mean they have demonstrated the ability in their current job, and they do that job exceptionally well. We would expect them to be in the top 10 percent of their peers. Along with that, they have to demonstrate the desire and orientation to be promoted to the job for which they are being considered. They need to see it as a real challenge and something that they want to do as a fulfillment for themselves. We look for people who have the track record in their current job, and people who have a great desire to go to the next level.

What does Art Lucas recommend to you as a strategy in your quest for promotion?

There are three things that I would recommend. Number one, do the job you're in now exceptionally well. If you're only average on that job, no matter what else you do, it really doesn't matter. So if you want to really get ahead, you have to be a top performer in what you are currently doing. Number two, volunteer outside of your own little niche to get involved in projects. Volunteer your time to be a mentor or a trainer or to serve on a project that is not in your current narrow niche. Show management your willingness to do other things. And number three, let people know that you have a desire for something else. Let them know that your goal is not to stay exactly where you currently are forever. Make it known you want to move to another level, and hopefully that level is something that the corporation needs. So find out what the corporation needs and let people know that's what you want to do.

FOUR

COMMUNICATION

Developing a strong inventory of communication skills is essential to career growth and success. Communication is the primary foundation of everything you do. No matter how good you perceive your communication skills to be, you can always improve. It's not uncommon for people to see themselves as excellent communicators and routinely blame others for any communication problems or breakdowns. We judge others harshly for not listening properly or ineffectively communicating their expectations, when in fact, it may actually be our delivery or reception of the message that is the impediment. Communication problems plague every organization, and those who learn to communicate effectively will rise to the top very quickly. Communication skills are transferable skills. Increasing your ability will positively impact every aspect of your life.

There are no other skills you use more, and as you will learn, being a good communicator is much more than just being a good talker! First we will look at sharpening your communications SAW.

Delivery of the Message

There are three styles of communication: aggressive, passive, and assertive. Communication breakdowns or disconnects frequently occur when aggressive or passive communication styles are used.

Aggressive Communication

Aggressive communication tends to be dominated by *you* statements that often infer blame, negative judgment, and place total responsibility on the other person. "*You* did this" or "*You* were supposed to do that." Aggressive communicators are often loud, intimidating, and frequent violators of spatial boundaries. They position themselves at very close range and display an in-your-face confrontational style. An aggressive communication style shuts down the listening function in others and results in defensiveness, resistance to the message, and preparation for challenge.

Aggressive communicators many times take blanket credit for all of the good things that have happened and are quick to tell you what they have accomplished, while frequently taking credit for others' work. Often they imply that the achievements of others would be impossible without their personal influence. While aggressive communicators may perceive themselves to be decisive leaders, their style frequently reduces the motivation of others and discourages collaboration and cooperation.

Passive Communication

Passive communication is devoid of interaction. These communicators share information with reluctance and only when necessary. Their delivery is incomplete, identifying only the issues of the moment, and rarely conveys the entire picture. Fragmentation is the norm. Passive communicators rarely initiate communication and are quick to offer blanket agreement with whatever is being said. This is demonstrated by their total absorption of information while offering little or no active feedback. Head nodding or verbal attends, such as, "uh huh, uh huh," are usually their only limited responses and there is no way to gauge comprehension. When on the receiving end, passive communicators frequently project the "deer in the headlights" stare, and you know that the lights are on but nobody is home! Passive communicators are also very quick to accept blame and may perceive that seeking *negative* responsibility is a successful method of appeasement and an effective way to end conversations or conflict. This style of communication is perceived by others as a sign of weakness, totally void of leadership and initiative. It does not contribute to promotability.

Assertive Communication

Assertive communication is conversational in tone. It is a signal of someone in control, showing no outward signs of negative emotion or judgment. Nonaccusatory *I* or *we* statements dominate. Instead of saying, "You said this . . . ", assertive communicators say, "What I heard was . . . ," and, instead of "You did this . . . ," they may say, "My perception of what happened is . . ." Assertive communicators accept responsibility, accountability, and recognize the achievements of others.

Assertive communication avoids the knee-jerk reaction, impulsive and emotionally charged responses of the aggressive style, and the typically subdued or withdrawn responses of the passive communicator. Assertive communication employs the appropriate use of time to think through a problem or issue before responding: "I don't want to respond reactively without thinking this through. Could we talk in an hour or so? I want to give your information the thought and complete attention that it deserves. Let me process it and we will meet again at (establishing a specific time for the follow-up)."

Assertive communication also avoids personalizing problems or issues. The focus is on *what* is being discussed, not *who* is actually presenting the information or *who* may have created the situation. While aggressive communicators typically personalize

selection, and your ability to frame your message for accurate comprehension, are major factors in your promotability.

The importance of vocabulary cannot be overemphasized. There is a lockstep relationship between the level of workplace success, upward mobility, and the command of the language. Standardized tests, psychological, aptitude, scholastic, or even civil service, all rely heavily on vocabulary as a measurement. You were tested and judged on your vocabulary throughout your years of formal education, and that testing and judgment continues as intensely and visibly each and every day in your workplace.

 Invest time and resources in the constant expansion of your vocabulary.

Typically, Americans communicate at the eighth or ninth grade level. Television programming, newspapers, and most periodicals present information at this level. It may be good enough for the mass media, but it is not good enough for you in your quest to be promoted.

Some suggestions for improving your verbal skills are:

- ◆ Strive to always maintain current awareness and usage of applicable, up-to-the-minute technical terms that are used in your industry and organization.
- ◆ Avoid talking down to people: communicate at their level of comprehension.
- ◆ Demonstrate a command of the vocabulary used at the organizational level where you seek promotion.
- ◆ Avoid jargon, codes, or buzzwords that may be unfamiliar to those you are communicating with, leaving them feeling intimidated or confused.
- ◆ Familiarize yourself with and use all the current idioms or nomenclature used to communicate internally within your group, team, department, and so on.
- ◆ Use as few words as possible. Never use two words when one will do.

Insuring You Are Understood

Delivering your message effectively is not enough. Communication is dysfunctional and breaks down if the message hasn't been accurately received. How can you insure that you have had an effective communication? Asking for a restatement of your message is by far the best tool at your disposal for measuring the effectiveness of your communication. While most of us are aware of this technique, few actually implement it, and those who do often use it ineffectively. Typically, we ask for restatement by saying, "Did you understand what I said?" (while bobbing our heads up and down to signal the answer that we're really looking for). Or we ask, "You don't have any questions, do you?" (while moving our heads back and forth clearly communicating our desire to discourage any questions). Predictably, receivers of our communication respond, "Oh yes, we understand" or "No, we don't have any questions." You walk away from the communication thinking, "This is great. They understood everything I said and they will follow up accordingly." The receivers frequently walk away muttering to themselves, "We have no idea what she just said and I don't have a clue as to what she expects." This miscommunication can be deadly, especially if there is a visible performance issue hanging in the balance.

These examples of the misuse of the restatement technique are very aggressive, relying heavily on *you*-based messages. This aggressive framing puts all the responsibility for accurate reception on the receivers and can be interpreted as a challenge to them to prove whether they understood. There is an implied visible embarrassment if, in fact, they cannot accurately restate the message.

What is the appropriate way to seek restatement? Ask listeners to repeat back to you, in their own words, their perception of the message. Apply an assertive, not aggressive, framework to your questions. "I want to be sure that I've done a good job of communicating. Help check me out. Summarize our communication." This method focuses on inclusion and interaction. You are asking listeners to check you out to determine your effectiveness as a communicator; this avoids negative judgment of them as listeners. It creates an environment where they can safely admit they didn't fully understand, and avoid the normal negative judgment or embarrassment that accompanies such a revelation. You are far better off determining communication breakdowns early—don't wait for lack of performance or unmet expectations to reveal poor comprehension.

Communication Assessment

	Yes	No
1. Do I communicate in either an aggressive or passive style?	☐	☐
2. Do I focus on the content of communications and avoid "personalizing" the messages?	☐	☐
3. Do I receive a large number of defensive responses from the people with whom I communicate?	☐	☐
4. Is my dress appropriate for the promotion level I am trying to achieve?	☐	☐
5. Do I dress in a way that is inappropriate, formal, informal, faddish, or generates negative attention?	☐	☐
6. Do I have a constant awareness of the impact of my nonverbal messages?	☐	☐
7. Do I discount the importance of voice quality, tone, pace, volume, and clarity?	☐	☐
8. Do I continually strive to improve my vocabulary and knowledge of organizational and industry specific terms?	☐	☐
9. Do I assume my communications are always received accurately, and fail to seek confirmation of comprehension?	☐	☐
10. My messages are always received accurately and I rarely experience frustration with others because "they just don't seem to get it."	☐	☐

Scoring:

Any *yes* responses to the odd-numbered questions or *no* responses to the even-numbered questions demand your attention and a plan for improvement to increase your promotability.

Being on the Receiving End

Effective listening is by far the least practiced of all communication skills. Most of us don't listen; we just wait to talk. We also listen selectively, filtering information to support opinions and perceptions that we have already formed. We "embrace the minutia" in communication, pouncing on the few things we disagree with rather than acknowledging the larger items of agreement. We hear what we expect or want to hear. If you think someone is an idiot, you tend to listen for the things he says to support that perception of idiocy. (You get to be right!) If you think someone is an expert in a certain area or you trust and respect him, you readily accept most things he says without question or challenge. Subjectivity, not objectivity, dominates our listening patterns.

Being an effective listener offers at least two advantages in your promotion pursuit.

1. Accurate comprehension reduces miscommunications, unmet expectations, and poor quality of work.
2. Effective listening builds strong and solid relationships and workplace alliances.

How can you become a more effective listener? Consider the following active listening techniques:

Become a Committed Listener

Listening is not something anyone does well instinctively. You must consistently rededicate yourself to the process. This is accomplished by constantly reestablishing the internal dialogue of, "I am going to listen to what people say and validate their right to opinions or perspectives that differ from mine. Not everyone thinks like I do. I can learn something from them."

This commitment also entails removing the major listening impediments of prejudging the value of the communicator and the validity of her thought process. This contributes to pre-rejection of her message because of *who* or *what* she is (different department, level, education, gender, race, age, etc.). The us-against-them mentality that permeates workplaces and personal lives leads to rejecting anything *they* have to say. Do not allow prejudice, diversity, rejection, or petty jealousies to hinder your effective listening.

 We listen best to the people who agree with us, however, we learn more from those who do not.

Clear the Decks

You must also physically prepare yourself to listen. Clear the immediate area of as many distractions or listening impediments as possible. If you are talking to someone face-to-face, turn off your computer screen, or at least turn it away unless it is an absolutely necessary part of your conversation. You will be tempted to divert your attention to the monitor (even the screensaver may catch your eye). If you are talking to someone and there are distractions in your line of sight behind him (an open hallway, a view into another office, or a window to the outside, etc.), reposition him and/or yourself to eliminate these distractions. People can actually see your lack of listening when they watch your attention shift to other things. This includes limiting interruptions and holding phone calls during important conversations. The momentum, impact, and accuracy of communication decline dramatically with each interruption. Consider moving to a neutral area (conference room, quiet corner, etc.) where potential interruptions can be minimized. Actively manage your listening environment.

Take Notes

Taking notes accomplishes three very important objectives.

1. You impress upon communicators the importance you place on *their* messages. This emphasizes your respect for them and the high value you place on their intellect and thought processes.
2. It forces you to become a more focused listener. Poised with pen in hand, you have to listen intently in order to have something to write down!
3. The accuracy and comprehension of the message are dramatically increased, and you have an informal written record for future reference.

Always explain your intention to take notes and ask permission. "This is really important and I want to take some notes to be sure I remember it accurately. Is that okay?" Asking permission puts the communicators at ease and gives them the opportunity to safely object if they so desire (which happens very rarely). Most people are flattered and impressed when they realize the importance you place on their messages.

This technique is also extremely effective for important telephone communications. We often display very poor telephone listening skills because we tend to do other things while listening (computer entry, reading/writing memos, eating lunch, etc.). Although we may not realize it, these distractions are very obvious to the people we are talking to and send a very negative message. How often do you hear people say, "Hello? Are you still there? Did you hear me? Did you understand what I just said?" This is perceived as proof and verification of the very low value you place on them and their communications. Always begin important phone conversations by saying, "This information is really important and I'm going to be taking some notes to insure my accuracy. If I'm behind a second or two in our conversation, I just want you to know why." Most people are so impressed they start to talk slower and louder!

Use Questions Appropriately

The use of questions is a valuable tool in the listening process. They not only prove to the communicator that you are paying attention, they allow you to refocus or regain control of the discussion if it tends to wander. Questions also provide the opportunity to seek clarifications of statements or data that are unclear.

Typical refocusing questions to try are:

"What do you think is the main issue here?"
"What do you see as the top three priorities?"
"We can deal with the side issues later. What is the best way I can help you with this right now?"

Typical questions for clarification are:

"I'm unclear on something. Did this happen one time, or does it occur repeatedly?"
"Did you say _____ or _____?"
"I'm not sure I understand these figures. Can you help me with them?"

Demonstrate You're Listening with Appropriate Verbal and Nonverbal "Attends"

Verbal attends are appropriate acknowledgments of messages and may include statements such as: "Uh huh," or "I see, that's very interesting." They may also be informal colloquialisms or buzzwords of the moment, such as "cool," "wow," or the like. Be wary of slang the higher you go in the organization. When communicating to the top, the fewer cutesy phrases the better. Effective verbal communication attends prove to communicators that you are focused on and grasping what they are saying.

You know what it looks like when people are listening to you effectively. They maintain eye contact, nod their heads appropriately, lean or sit slightly forward toward you, and give you their full attention. Obviously, these are the same visuals you must display when you are receiving messages. Smiling in response to a statement, or raising your eyebrows when a particularly salient point is made, are powerful indicators of a riveted listener. Lack of eye contact, staring at the ceiling, playing with a paper clip, or doodling doesn't impress people that you are listening intently to what they are saying!

Testing Your Listening Accuracy

Initiate feedback/check for understanding. By far, the most effective listening technique is the tried-and-true summary in your own words. It shows your understanding of the communication. "Let me be sure that I've heard this correctly. What I heard is . . . Is that correct?" (Please note the assertive, not aggressive, phrasing—the accusatory *you* is not utilized.)

Your quick, effective summary demonstrates at least three things:

1. Your comprehension of the message (or lack thereof)
2. Proof of your active listening
3. The importance you place on the communication

If you summarize correctly, the communicator will agree and you will both have confidence in knowing that there was an accurate transfer of information. If your summary is inaccurate, there is an opportunity to correct any misunderstanding. In cases such as these, you can merely say, "Obviously, I didn't understand the entire message. Please let me hear it once again."

If your summaries are greeted by glazed looks or puzzled appearances, chances are the communicators have no clue as to what you have just said. (Poor listening skills travel in both directions.) They may have been so intent on what *they* were saying, that they weren't able to switch gears and process your response (a common occurrence). Do not make the mistakes of interpreting this as agreement or allowing it to go uncorrected. Do not move on until you have effectively resolved the miscommunication.

Effective summaries are not just "parroting" back, word-for-word, exactly what was said. Some very intelligent birds and many less intelligent people are capable of doing this! This demonstrates only the hearing of words but not actual comprehension. Putting it in your own terminology truly demonstrates an accurate understanding of the message.

Listening Assessment

On a scale of 1 to 5 (1 = never; 5 = always), rate your listening skills. An honest assessment will allow you to identify your personal strengths, weaknesses, and action steps needed for improvement. Not rating yourself honestly and accurately will result in perpetuating your listening status quo and maintaining significant internal roadblocks to promotion.

I listen as much as or less than I talk.   _____

I am able to focus on what's being said without becoming distracted.   _____

I listen patiently, allowing others to finish their communications before adding my comments or responses.   _____

I have a high level of interest in what's being said.   _____

I overcome my boredom when listening to the conversations of others.   _____

I listen to everyone equally regardless of their position, age, gender, race, and so on.   _____

I am always open to diverse opinions, especially those different from my own.   _____

I can accurately recall conversations an hour after their conclusion.   _____

I give full and complete attention, both verbally and nonverbally, to the people with whom I am communicating.   _____

I am aware of the nonverbal messages I send to others.   _____

I acknowledge when I do not understand a
communication.   _____

My words, tone of voice, and nonverbals are always
aligned in support of the message I intend to send.   _____

I do not preform judgments of what other people
are saying and I refrain from forming my
conclusion until they have completed their
communications.   _____

I take notes of all important conversations.   _____

I look for areas of agreement and de-emphasize
disagreements.   _____

Scoring:

Less than 44: Significant development of listening skills is
necessary.

45–60: This is typical—indicating some effective listening
skills and room for improvement.

61–68: This indicates extremely effective listening capability.

69 and above: Look up the word *reality* in the dictionary!

Breaking Through the Listening Barriers of Others

If people are preoccupied with other issues or their barriers
to listening are in full force, there are specific techniques you
can use to alleviate the situation.

◆ **Pause for effect.** If people are obviously not listening, do
not continue to talk. The pregnant pause becomes very obvious
to them and encourages them to refocus on your message. Stop
talking until the receiver becomes aware of the silence.

◆ **Reposition yourself.** Shift position to eliminate any
distractions they may see behind you or move closer to them in
a nonmenacing fashion to achieve more communication closeness.

◆ **Gesture.** If their eyes are wandering, place an upwardly
pointed index finger in their line of sight. When they begin to
focus on your movement, slowly bring it back to just under

your chin. This causes them to follow the movement and refocus on you.

◆ **Ask people to take notes.** Say to them, "Do me a favor and take a couple of quick notes" or "Please write this down for me." You will be amazed at how many people do exactly what you tell them. They will pick up their pens and begin to write.

◆ **Reschedule.** If someone truly is preoccupied and other priorities may be overriding your message, discretion may be the better part of valor. Acknowledge this and generate an agreement to meet at a specific time in the very near future. "Courtney, I know this is not a good time for you. Could we get together in thirty minutes?" or "I know this isn't a good time, let's get together immediately after lunch."

The Four Ps

There are many opportunities for you to impact the perceptions others have of your communication abilities. Among the most significant are:

Written Communication

Written communication is an excellent opportunity for you to showcase your communication skills. While verbal communications are short-lived, one-time events, written communications continue their visibility. Many memos, letters, and so on, take on lives of their own. Written communication can be a double-edged sword. Effectively written and implemented, it can positively influence your career, however, it can also work against you if written or used inappropriately. Here are some things to keep in mind about written communication.

Using grammar correctly is of paramount importance. Nothing detracts from written communication or imbeds an immediate negative impression as deeply as grammatical errors. While today's computer software technology is helpful, do not fall into the complacent trap of assuming total accuracy. Grammar and spell check software programs don't catch everything. Even with the current technology, consider these three suggestions: Edit. Edit. Edit. Are you getting the point here? Keep this in mind—the only differences between celibate and celebrate are an *i* and an *r* . . . and these little letters really change the message!

Written communication must be concise. Don't write a book, nobody wants to read one. Keep written communications to as few pages as possible, preferably one. The guide for written communication is quality, not quantity. Winston Churchill is reported to have said to an aide who placed a three-inch-high report on his desk, "That report, by its very size, demands that it will never be read." Reading your written communication should not be perceived as punishment or an exercise in endurance.

Seek opportunities to put any positive information in writing. If you are thanking or congratulating someone, reporting successes (major and minor), recommending solutions, providing updates, and the like, all of these should be in writing whenever possible. Insure accuracy, provide proof when available or necessary, and distribute the communication as widely as possible.

Be wary of putting any negative information in writing—avoid it if possible, and do so only when requested by someone in authority (your boss). Never put any negative information in writing that is not supported by verifiable fact. If it is opinion or perception, communicate it verbally. Written negative communication is generally targeted at individuals or at a specific area of responsibility for which someone will be held accountable. Others will pore over your communication looking for alleged inaccuracies or biased perceptions. Inaccurate, negative written communication can sit in someone's file and become a weapon to be used against you for years to come. Enemies created in writing tend to have long life spans. Negative written communication is a time bomb waiting to go off when you least expect it.

Your communication style can be unique or conform with the culture of the organization, however, never allow your style to violate the organization's boundaries or norms of what is acceptable. There are many resources for improving your writing abilities if you so desire. One excellent guideline is, "Write just as you speak," employing the same style to convey messages in writing as you do verbally. Word selection, length, tone, and so on, should all be consistent in both written and verbal communications.

Guidelines for Written Communication

◆ Be concise.
◆ Surface your message early—you're not writing a novel, get away from having a beginning, middle, end—state your point and get out.
◆ Avoid anger. Be polite and never vent emotionally in writing.
◆ Never fall into the trap of putting "he said/she said" in writing.
◆ Avoid jargon, slang, or technical terms that may be unknown or misunderstood by your reader.
◆ Be clear, don't call a paper clip a "thin material fastening device."
◆ Avoid embellishment; unsubstantiated claims tend to turn readers off.

Document Success

 Seize every opportunity to put any examples of personal success in writing.

When you have successfully completed a project, accomplished a specific task, achieved a goal relating to your performance appraisal, or effectively supported someone else in a successful accomplishment, seek ways to put this information in writing. Whenever possible, route these to your boss and/or other promotion decision makers or influencers. At the very least, have these documented successes available for your next performance appraisal. These communications should be supported by accurate, factual data whenever possible. Some examples are:

"Dear Boss: As we discussed, the information was sent to all of the AT&T locations by Friday at 2:30. Attached is a copy of all the contact people, and their locations, who received the mailing."

OR

"Jim asked me for some detailed information to help close the deal with General Motors. It took almost two hours to put it together, and by using the information, he was able to close the deal. He did a great job." (Copy of the confirmation letter attached.)

OR

"The team had committed to completing the ABC project by the end of the month. I wanted to let you know that not only is it done, it was completed five days early. You may want to let the team know how much you appreciate their efforts."

Don't Wait to Be Told

Do not sit back and expect people to automatically bring information to you. Don't passively fall prey to being left out of the loop. Actively seek data and information. "Nobody told me" is the anthem of blamers and losers. Your information flow shouldn't be dependent upon what others remember to tell you. Actively pursue the information. Do so assertively, never confrontationally, and trust your instincts. If you sense something is happening or developing, dig deep to find out about it.

If you find yourself being left out of the loop, develop an informal log to document your "loop gaps." Identify trends of topics, reports, types, or sources of information that may not be flowing to you smoothly. If it happens repeatedly, begin to analyze the source of, or the impediment to, the flow of information. If you sense a trend, diagnose the root cause and seek correction. These are usually easy fixes once they are analyzed properly.

An effective way to present this would be: "I've identified a pattern of not receiving (this specific information) on a timely basis. What can we do to eliminate future problems and insure that I get the information that I need?"

Presentation Skills

Visibly showcase your talents by seizing every opportunity to present information in front of a group. If there is training to be done, volunteer to do it. If an idea is to be presented, always attempt to be the one making the presentation (giving full credit to others who may have had input). If there is an opportunity to make any type of presentation to a customer, leader, internal employees, team, or department, take advantage of it if possible. Successful group presentations allow you to demonstrate your skills and knowledge to a large number of people at one time. It would take an enormous amount of time and opportunity to achieve this exposure on an individual basis. Effective group presentations increase your promotability and catapult you ahead of your competition.

While group presentations are tremendous opportunities, they generate high levels of fear and anxiety for many. The anxiety of speaking in front of a group has been identified by some as the number one fear in the American workplace. The fear is usually based in the potential for public embarrassment. We fear getting up in front of a group and making fools of ourselves. The key to overcoming that fear and making powerful presentations is practice and preparation. Don't let this fear deny you valuable opportunities for visibility.

Acknowledge Mistakes and Responsibility Appropriately

When you are in a position to take responsibility for a mistake, always do so quickly and effectively. The sooner you acknowledge it, the sooner it will be over; the longer you wait, the more the problem may compound itself. A sagacious leader once said, "Bring me a problem early and I am your ally, consultant and advocate. Bring me a problem too late, and I may well be your antagonist and executioner."

Here are some guidelines for acknowledging mistakes and taking responsibility:

◆ **Clearly take responsibility.** Do not talk around it, attempt to blur facts, or convey a lack of willingness to accept accountability.

◆ **Avoid blaming.** Do not inappropriately distance yourself from responsibility. Taking someone down with you is not an attractive behavior.

◆ **Identify the learning.** In a clear and concise manner, communicate what you have learned from the event. Be wary of self-serving learning statements that may work against you. Avoid: "I learned never to trust anyone but myself" or "I learned that if I want the job done right, I have to do it myself because others can't be trusted." These are nothing more than sly attempts at shifting blame. Appropriate responses might be, "I learned to be more diligent in monitoring results" or "I learned that it's necessary to do a more thorough job of follow-up."

◆ **Identify future corrective behavior.** Simply stated, acknowledge what you will *do* differently in the future. "In the future, I will develop early warning signs to get quicker feedback if there is a problem."

Communicating Bad News

Here are some key points to help in communicating bad news.

◆ **Disseminate the news quickly but thoughtfully.** The longer you procrastinate, the worse the message becomes. If the bad news isn't communicated quickly, chances are good the rumor mill will kick in and generate the information in a distorted, probably even more damaging form. This is never to your advantage.

◆ **Clearly differentiate between assumptions and facts.** If you know something to be true, provide detailed documentation. If you are making an assumption, clearly identify it as such. Avoid: "This is what's going to happen" and rephrase it as "Here is a potential problem we need to consider." Do not allow your perceptions, predictions, or assumptions to be interpreted as facts.

◆ **Always offer corrective alternatives.** Never communicate bad news and leave it hanging. Always lessen the damage of the bad news by offering suggestions for corrective action. Many leaders are frequently heard to say, "Don't bring me problems, bring me solutions." Don't wait for them to ask, have your recommendations developed. Frequently, we avoid communicating bad news because we fear being the target of "shoot the messenger" reactions. In reality, messengers get shot because they bring only bad news. They survive and thrive when they offer solutions. Even though the solutions may not be implemented, they can serve as the basis for creative problem solving.

Present yourself as a source of solutions, always linking negative communications with positive options.

Some of the best opportunities to showcase your promotable talent may have their roots in bad news, negative events, problems, or crises. Seize every opportunity to impress others with your problem-solving ability. Reinforcing prophecies of gloom and doom or feeding the frenzy of negativity over problems is counterproductive. Become the calming, solving force in the turmoil of bad news.

The Responsibilities of Reporting

Organizational alignment requires that you bear specific responsibility for reporting to the people above you. While much of our reporting activity in today's workplace has degenerated to "proving to me that you have been busy" as opposed to actually demonstrating productivity, it is nonetheless a necessary evil. To enhance your promotability, do not buck the reporting system.

Always submit reports on a timely basis. Your reports *may* go unread, but *someone* is probably responsible for keeping a log to determine the responsiveness and timeliness of your report submissions.

Determine your boss's preferred style of reporting. What information does she require? How does she want to receive it? What information does she find meaningless or excessive?

 Find out what your boss wants to know and present it to her in a format she wants to receive.

Report only what is necessary and be prepared to offer additional supporting information if requested. Just because you have a volume of information available does not mean that it all must be reported. Report concisely, and expand only if requested to do so.

Real-World Promotion Mentoring

Priscilla Hall is a technical training supervisor for Alcon Labs in Ft. Worth, Texas. Alcon Labs is one of the largest pharmaceutical companies in the world, specializing in the research, development, and manufacture of quality eye-care products.

Priscilla shared her thoughts on the importance of communication in the promotion process.

One of the most important things in business for being promoted is communication, communication, communication. It's by far the number one factor. Every time I see an e-mail with misspelled words, it has a negative impact. I don't think people realize that communication, such as e-mail, literally shows your personality. It's proof of your literacy skills and an example of your ability to communicate. If you are a person who provides volumes of information when a short, concise answer will do, you really need to go back and revisit your communication skills.

Regarding the challenges facing people seeking promotion in today's workplace, Priscilla said:

Organizations are becoming a lot flatter. Promotions are just not happening as often as they used to. What we see in manufacturing is a lot of people are being developed into higher-level, nonexempt roles, such as group leaders, which are assistant-type positions. But actual full promotions into management or supervisory level positions are not happening as frequently. Also, a lot of jobs now require that you have more than one specific skill. In our particular field, not only do you have to have good technical expertise, you also have to have leadership or administrative skills, a good business sense, and, extremely important today, are priority management and project management skills. Along with organizations becoming flatter, the global network, the importance of information systems, and the Internet are going to be extremely important in the future. Understanding the Internet, the ability to efficiently use the information that comes from these resources, is a valuable skill. Anyone who has a good handle on this type of information is very comfortable with computer systems, and I'm not just talking about the ability to do word processing or use spreadsheet formats, but being able to use the Internet to gather research information. This is going to be very important in the long run.

Priscilla also had some interesting suggestions on the importance of networking.

Learning to expand your sphere of influence is very important. Volunteering to be on a Christmas party committee, or demonstrating that you are willing to do a little bit more or go beyond your current scope, is something that demonstrates to people that you want to get things done. It's also very important to have a positive rather than a negative approach. If you are the kind of person that every time somebody voices an idea or recommends a change, your first response is, "Oh, that can't be done" or "We've already done that before," you are positioning yourself very negatively. If you are an individual who gives the appearance and proves the fact that you are a "can-do" person and you want opportunities, then if just given a chance, you can make things happen. That attitude really pushes your promotability. If you are in a large organization, get to know people in various divisions. Seek opportunities to join cross-functional teams. Many organizations have outside projects within the community, perhaps things such as Junior Achievement, the United Way, and so on. These are tremendous opportunities to unite with other people from the organization, build your network, and gain valuable experience. If there is a softball team or a sports team, support it. You can't imagine how many different types of people from all levels of the organization you can meet and get to know in these activities. Also, take advantage of all corporate training programs. This gives you another valuable opportunity to meet people and increase the influence of your network.

FIVE

ORGANIZATIONAL SKILLS

Much of your efficiency and productivity hinges upon your organizational skills. While critical to success, these skills typically are not widely or effectively taught in the workplace. In this chapter we will discuss what skills you must have and how to develop them, as well as how to insure these skills are visible to the promotion decision makers.

As we look at sharpening your organizational SAW we will address the importance of establishing goals, planning, and careful prioritization. We will also offer very specific strategies for becoming more visibly organized.

Goal Setting

Organization begins with the establishment of goals. People who establish goals are much more productive than those who do not. Goals establish objectives and organizational skills are the tools used to achieve success. You must organize yourself and your activities to accomplish your goals.

It's important to identify two distinct sets of goals: your personal goals as well as your organizational goals. You alone determine your personal goals, while organizational goals are usually determined by others. You must develop specific personal goals concerning your personal productivity and performance, along with your promotion goals. These goals must be specific, reasonable, and attainable. The organization's goal may be a 10 percent increase in productivity. Your personal goal may be to exceed a 10 percent increase in productivity *and* be promoted within the next eighteen months. The probability of your promotability increases when your personal and organizational goals are aligned. When your personal and organizational goals are not aligned or supportive of each other, then a realistic organizational opportunity for advancement probably doesn't exist.

Key questions: Do you know what the overall organizational goals are? Do you know what goals have been set for you? Do you know what you are being specifically held accountable for? If not, go find out!

 You cannot be organized until you know what you are trying to accomplish.

There are many recognized models for successful goal setting. Some attempt to take a very simple exercise and compound it into a complex task. The simpler the better. An effective empirical goal-setting model asks the following questions:

◆ **What are you going to do?** This must be very specific. You can't just get *better*. *Better* is much too general and can't be measured. You must increase (or decrease) productivity by X percent. The more specific the goal, the greater the possibility it will be achieved.

◆ **Why do you want to do it?** Is it relevant? Does it support your overall plan and further your personal and organizational agendas?

◆ **When are you going to do it?** All goals must have a timeline. A goal without a timeline is nothing more than a wish.

◆ **How will you know when you've done it?** This addresses

measurement. The more specific and objective the measurement, the more successful the outcome. Subjective measurements rely on opinions, and opinions are relative, relegating success merely to subjective perception, which is always open to debate.

♦ **Have you increased your commitment by putting your goals into writing?** Goals must also be in writing and shared. Putting them in writing emphasizes your commitment, sharing them with others makes your commitment public and gives others permission to help monitor your success.

 A goal that isn't shared is a secret.

Goal Setting and Risk Taking

There is an element of risk in the establishment and sharing of goals. Goal setting itself is a positive statement proclaiming your expectations of growth and achievement. Establishing goals diminishes the status quo and publicly proclaims your pursuit of change. All of this involves risk, and with any risk comes the possibility of failure. It is easier and safer to avoid risk and dismiss the goal-setting process. You are much more in control of today's status quo than tomorrow's change. Goal setting is a positive statement about future achievement. The first step of any journey is determining the destination, and effective goal setting is that first step. Are you willing to take the goal-setting risk?

Prioritizing

Once goals have been established, it is important to prioritize your tasks and activities. What tasks are most critical to the achievement of your personal and organizational goals? Tasks and activities can be broken down into four areas.

Category 1: Critical Tasks of Today

These are the duties in your job description, and the crises, problems, and deadline driven projects that are your responsibility. These are the tasks and activities that support the efforts of today—keeping the wheels of the organization turning, generating revenue, meeting compliance requirements, and so on. Critical tasks are very important and are the reasons you were hired and are still employed. If you are good at accomplishing these tasks, you are highly capable and get to keep your job!

Category 2: The Developmental Tasks of Tomorrow

These tasks and activities address growth, development, and change. Typically they include planning, preparation, relationship-building, evaluation, and training. While we recognize their importance, they are frequently left undone because they lack any urgency at the moment. Although they are extremely important, they don't cry out "do me now." These are the things we intend to accomplish but never have the time. During your last performance appraisal, you probably said to your boss, "The things I really wanted to accomplish but just wasn't able to were . . . " These were probably the developmental tasks of tomorrow. Truly successful people discipline themselves to invest an appropriate amount of their time to addressing these critical tasks of tomorrow. If you are good at accomplishing these tasks, you get promoted!

Category 3: Busywork

These tasks and activities make huge demands on our time, frequently appear to be urgent, but are relatively nonessential to the overall accomplishment of personal or organizational goals. Often they fall under the dreaded category of "other duties as assigned." (Every job description contains a similar catchall phrase that serves as a safety net for management. It basically states, "Also included in your job description is anything else that I decide to assign to you and you never get to say 'that's not my job'. It becomes your job merely upon my request.") Often included in this busywork category are tasks delegated to us by others—they do not have time to do them so they send them along to us. This busywork often comes to us over the telephone and may be the result of someone else's poor planning.

Interestingly, much of the reporting we are required to do in today's workplace is actually Category 3, busywork. Many people invest significant amounts of time in compiling reports that no one else ever reads! Checklists are maintained to document report submission or tardiness, though no one ever bothers to read the content. They know if your report is late, but they cannot tell you what is in it! If you can accurately identify the busywork components of your reporting requirements, you may be able to make recommendations for elimination or restructuring, resulting in a more effective and less time-consuming reporting format.

 Do not object to reporting, only attempt to minimize effort and maximize impact!

The more busywork you can eliminate, the more time you free up for promotion pursuit. If you are good at Category 3 busywork, you are very busy and probably stressed out!

Category 4: Time wasters

These are the things we do to waste our time or the time of others. Typically, this includes abusing break privileges, misusing the telephones or computer systems, extended leisurely lunches, and chatting, venting, or whining sessions. If you are good at Category 4 time wasters, you will probably get fired . . . not promoted!

The Promotion Formula

In a perfect world, you would spend 80 percent of your time on Category 1; 20 percent of your time on Category 2; and 0 percent of your time on Categories 3 and 4. In the real world, Categories 3 and 4 become the battleground. You *cannot* reduce the time that you spend on Category 1, because these tasks are critical and must be accomplished. Therefore, the only way to increase your time on Category 2 tasks (those most positively impacting your promotability), is to reduce Category 3 as much as possible, and eliminate Category 4.

If you are going to do more with less, you must apply your time and efforts more efficiently by waging war against Category 3 and 4 activities.

A Promotion-Enhancing Exercise

For a minimum of two weeks (ten working days), develop a working inventory of your tasks. When you work on a specific task, analyze which of the four categories it falls under. Honesty and accuracy are essential. Note the task and the approximate time expended.

Once you have categorized your tasks, you will begin to see the emergence of a pattern. Focus on reducing, not eliminating. Once you have a list of the busywork, efficiency drainers, sit down with your boss, share your perceptions, and negotiate adjustments. You won't be able to eliminate all of the Category 3 activities, however, you may be surprised at how much they can actually be reduced.

Many times the line between Categories 1 and 3 becomes very blurry. Because most Category 3 tasks seem to be highly urgent, they are automatically considered Category 1, though this may not be the case. A great way to determine the difference between Categories 1 and 3 is to ask yourself the *magic question of life*, which is "What's the worst thing that can happen if this task isn't done?" If the answer does not contain the words death, bleeding, or termination, it may be a Category 3 task!

Planning

Planning is something everyone gives lip service to, but in reality, few do it effectively. Lack of planning promotes the eternal chaos of being very busy, constantly reacting to crises, and allowing tasks to manage you instead of you managing them.

If you don't plan, you don't have a job, the job has you!

There are many guides, programs, and tools for planning. Some are so complex they require extensive investment and special training just to use them. Many people plan effectively with nothing more than legal pad notes maintained on a daily basis. There are many very effective computer programs to help you to gain and maintain planning control. How you do it is up to you. The important thing is to do it, and the simpler the better. Any effective planning program must contain the following components: an extensive to-do list, alignment of time slots and tasks, and anticipation of the predictable unknown.

To-Do List

Every daily plan must begin with a detailed accounting of everything to be done that day and the approximate time needed for each activity (including going to lunch). This to-do list is always very lengthy and leads to the realization that you will have more to do than you have time to do it in! This is when prioritization becomes critical. Assess your to-do list by ranking each task in one of the four categories.

Once this prioritization is completed, ask yourself these three key questions:

1. **What can I eliminate?** (What really falls into Categories 3 or 4 that doesn't actually have to be done at all?)
2. **What can I delay?** (The delay *must* include a future target date for completion. Failing to set a specific follow-up means the task will remain undone and could become a threatening crisis at a later date.)
3. **What can I delegate?** (Is there anyone above, equal to,

or below me in the organization who I can assign this
task to or ask for help?)

This exercise is not easy and forces you to make some tough
decisions concerning your commitments of time and resources.
Exercise diligence to insure your commitments accomplish your
personal goals of performance and promotability, and support
the overall objectives of your boss and other promotion decision
makers and influencers. If you do not prioritize effectively, you
will allow some of the less important busywork tasks to demand
your time and attention while leaving some critical Category 1
and 2 tasks uncompleted.

Align Time Slots and Tasks

The next step in the planning process is to allot a specific
time to accomplish each of your objectives. Along with determining what you are going to do, you have to identify when
you are going to do it. Time considerations should reflect work
process flow, predictable availability of resources (including people), and your personal preferences and capabilities.

Analyze your energy cycle. Your critical tasks and those that
most impact your promotability should be scheduled when you
typically are the most productive, creative, and focused. Everyone has an energy cycle. Some are morning people, while others are late afternoon or evening people, and some haven't
found their energy cycles yet!

The illustration at the top of page 99 depicts the typical energy cycle of those considered to be morning people. They are at
their peak of energy, creativity, and productivity between 8 A.M.
and 12 noon, and experience a severe decline immediately after
lunch. Obviously, they should plan to do their most challenging, creative, promotion-enhancing tasks early in the workday.
Typically, however, these people will not plan their energy cycle effectively. They may arrive early, dive into their in-baskets,
and accomplish many of their less challenging or busywork ac-

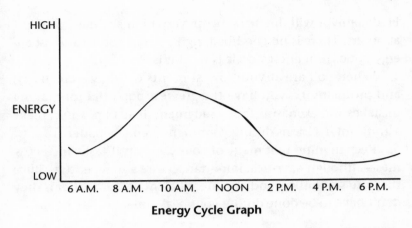

Energy Cycle Graph

tivities before noon. Accomplishing lots of little things results in a feeling of achievement (quantity, not quality!), but they are applying their most productive time to their least challenging tasks. When they have available time in the afternoon, they are experiencing their predictable lull and aren't capable of producing their most creative work. They would be much better off dedicating their morning hours to the challenging Category 1 and 2 tasks.

A Promotion-Enhancing Exercise

Starting at the extreme left portion of the empty graph that follows, track your typical energy level throughout the day.

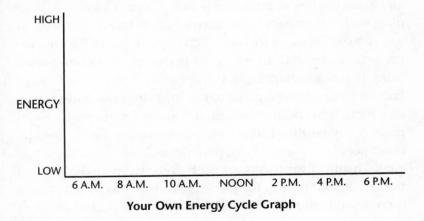

Your Own Energy Cycle Graph

Predictably it will fluctuate, being very high at times, very low at others. There is no good/bad, right/ wrong, or better/best energy cycle. Your energy cycle is what it is!

When you are at your lowest points of energy, creativity, and productivity, you have the greatest potential for making mistakes and exercising faulty judgment. If at all possible, make significant decisions during your highest energy patterns.

Keep in mind that many of your Category 1 tasks and activities—although of critical importance—are also repetitive. Since they are so familiar and you are efficient at doing them, they don't have to be done during your peak time.

Knowing your boss's predictable energy cycle can be valuable for determining when to present information, ask for guidance, or seek approval.

Anticipate the Predictable Unknown

Surprise! Surprise! Surprise! You do not have total control over all of your time. While we all lament the negative impact of interruptions and disruptions on our productivity, we curiously ignore their reality when we plan. We try to schedule ourselves as if we had total control over every minute of every day, and when the first interruption or unforeseen crisis destroys our plan, we fall right back into reactive daily behavior.

To avoid these perpetual reactive patterns, build time for predictable disruptions into your planning. You know something is going to happen to disrupt your plan, you just don't know who or what it is going to be. The disruption is inevitable! Plan for it. It has been estimated that somewhere between 40–70 percent of your time is taken away from you and controlled by other people or events (boss, peers, crises, deadlines, meetings, etc.). To adjust for this, start off by selectively dedicating 50 percent of your time to the predictable unknown by scheduling incremental amounts of "flex time" into your schedule. Flex time is encumbered, but unassigned time that is available for absorbing the inevitable disruptions inherent in your workday. This strategy faces the reality that you can only effectively plan for 50 percent of your day. This puts significant pressure on your ability to prioritize your tasks. You will have to make some difficult decisions as to what takes priority, and what must be eliminated, delayed, or delegated. You can bury your head in the sand and hope, pray, and assume that you will get it all done, or deal with the actual amount of time controlled by you. The following is an illustration of a typical morning plan.

08:00–08:15	Finish monthly report
08:15–08:30	" " " " "
08:30–08:45	Approve pending requisitions
08:45–09:00	" " " " "
09:00–09:15	**Flex time**
09:15–09:30	Restructuring project meeting
09:30–10:00	" " " " "
10:00–10:15	" " " " "
10:15–10:30	**Flex time**
10:30–10:45	" " "
10:45–11:00	Return phone messages
11:00–11:15	Reconcile statements
11:15–11:30	" " " " "
11:30–11:45	**Flex time**
11:45–12:00	" " "

Sample Morning Plan

In this example, 1¼ hours of the morning schedule is dedicated to flex time and made available to absorb interruptions, crisis eruptions, and the like. Typically, your boss may call and say, "I need to talk with you." You now have two options:

1. Say, "I've got some time between 9:00 and 9:15. How does that sound?" (Using the available flex time to schedule the discussion.)

2. You can respond immediately to your boss knowing that you can utilize the 9:00 to 9:15 flex time to complete the monthly report. (Responding immediately may increase your promotability.)

Either way the boss's unforeseen interruption does not totally disrupt your morning plan. Flex time is dispersed intermittently throughout the day. Have some flex time available when you are at your high energy peak and some available when you are at your lower points of energy and creativity. (It is probably not wise to dedicate flex time to your *lowest* energy point of the day. This could turn into a nap!!)

Your promotability is best served by efficiently utilizing the 50 percent of your time that you do control rather than stressfully agonizing over the 50 percent that you can't control.

Evaluation

Goal setting and planning, supported by effective prioritizing, are critical organizational skills, and paramount in your quest for a promotion. It is also necessary to take time to routinely evaluate the success of these efforts (this is a Category 2 activity!) to assess:

- ◆ Are my current goals still valid?
- ◆ Have additional goals/responsibilities emerged?
- ◆ Are my priorities still in alignment?
- ◆ Have new priorities changed the emphasis of my efforts?
- ◆ Have my behavior and focus been adjusted to accommodate change?
- ◆ Does my planning support my goals and priorities?
- ◆ Do I plan and focus effort on achieving my Category 2 promotion-impacting tasks?

- ◆ Do my overall behaviors, actions, and applications of my time support my plan, priorities, and goals?
- ◆ Am I majoring in the minors?
- ◆ Have I allowed myself to become sidetracked?

The absence of evaluation broadens the ever-widening gap between performance and intention, and results in activities and behaviors that are not aligned with your goals and priorities. If you fail to evaluate, you tend to spin your wheels on unproductive pursuits, and after an extended period of time, begin to realize that while your goal was to arrive in the Florida Keys, you wound up in Alaska and can't understand how it happened! The lack of evaluation means continuously making the same mistakes, entrenching the status quo, and is the mother of "caught in a rut" behaviors.

Appropriate evaluation means taking the time to look at the career road signs and making sure you are still on the right highway.

The key to evaluation lies in answering the question, "Is what I am doing really paying off and giving me the results that I want?" Evaluation can be painful because it requires taking personal responsibility for your stated goals and objectives, which aren't necessarily supported by your behaviors and activities.

Personal Organization

Some people are inherently more organized than others. Some are trained, though most are not. Some live in an orderly universe, while others are submerged in constant disorganization. Most proclaim to be organized, and even the most disorganized give lip service to the fact that they really are in control and that there is a method to their chaotic madness.

Some people may actually con themselves into believing their chaos is somehow orderly and they fail to acknowledge the negative message their disorganization sends to others. The perception of others that you are out of control and unable to manage your current workload, could have an insurmountable, long-term, negative impact on your career growth.

Reclaim Control: "Defeating the Desk Demon"

How do you clean up a disastrously disorganized desk and maintain organization? Follow this proven ten-step process:

Step 1: Plan the time and equip yourself for the task. Dedicate a minimum of three hours of uninterrupted time (some desks/offices/cubicles may take more). This must be a specific block of time and may require an evening or weekend to eliminate interruptions.

You will need:

- ◆ Lots of file folders
- ◆ File folder labels
- ◆ Three multicolored markers (pick your favorite colors)
- ◆ Legal pad
- ◆ Wastebasket

Step 2: Clear a place on the floor next to your desk or work station, large enough for two separate piles of paper.

Step 3: Systematically, one item at a time, pick up every piece of paper on your desk, floor, chairs, bookcases, or any other visible surface. For each piece of paper, ask yourself this key question, "Is this paper dead or alive?"

Step 4: Place each piece of paper in one of the two piles on the floor: the "dead" pile (closest to the wastebasket) or the "alive" pile. As you go through this lengthy process, you will begin to discover the dead pile grows much larger than the alive pile. You will probably find memos from people who resigned, retired, or passed away two years ago. Do *not* just toss the dead papers away individually. It is very important for you to imprint the size of the dead pile on your brain. When this step is completed, you will have a clean desk, chairs, bookcase, and so on, and two piles of paper on your floor.

Step 5: Conduct a dignified funeral and bury the dead pile in the wastebasket. (You may need two if the basket overfloweth!)

Step 6: Bring the alive pile to the top of your desk.

Step 7: Pick up each piece of paper in the alive pile and ask yourself two questions.

1. What should I do with this?
2. How will I file it?

Step 8: Log and number your responses on a legal pad. List the entries on your legal pad in the order in which they occur. Do *not* attempt to prioritize or categorize them and *do not take any follow-up action*. The following illustration demonstrates this process.

Tasks/what?	File
1. Memo to Sam/benefit package	Sam
2. Request to join MIS association	Associations
3. Get P.O. for software	Purchasing
4. Research delinquent reimbursement check	Benefits

Step 8 Entries

After each entry, pick up a file folder, put the paper inside, and attach a label identified in accordance with the designation on your legal pad. It is extremely important for your file folder label and legal pad to be consistent. Place the folder into a file system as close to your desk or workspace as possible. When you have this completed, you will have a clean desk, a legal pad that becomes your inventory of tasks, and a bulging, obese filing system. Congratulations!

Step 9: Now prioritize your inventory of tasks (the legal pad!) by color coding it with your markers. Designate three colors of your choice to identify:

> Hot = immediate, important, must be done now
> Warm = important but not immediate or urgent
> Tepid = when you get around to it

When you have prioritized your entire list, you will have an organized plan of what you have to do and the order of task importance. This process is equally effective in dealing with e-mail backlogs. Add each incoming request or task to your list, delete, and move on!

Step 10: Establish a goal to retire a specific number of items from your inventory of tasks each day. (*Important note*: Do *not* attempt to retire all of the tasks at one time. This does not change your long-term behavior. You have done this many times before, clearing off your desk in a great burst of energy only to become mired in chaos again as the process repeats itself and the clutter blossoms.) This ten-step technique is intended to change your inefficient behavior. If you have one hundred items in your inventory of tasks, perhaps a goal of ten per day would be reasonable. In theory, you would retire the entire list in ten days. (That's not quite how it works, however!) In reality, you will be adding more items each day and your goal must be to retire more tasks than you typically contribute each day.

Address your hot items first. Always retire your hot color designations before you move on to warm and then to tepid. Hot colors always take priority.

As you complete an item on your list, cross it off, recycle the file folder, and always take time to congratulate yourself on becoming the new, in control, organized, and efficient you.

Maintain Control

Once the chaos has been contained, it is critical to maintain day-to-day control. You must prevail in the daily "battle of the in-box." The in-box (and incoming e-mail) are really the enemy. They are the source of your disorganization. To gain victory, you must practice the sunset rule. The sunset rule states: "The sun always sets in the west over an *empty* in-box and *deleted* e-mail file."

At the conclusion of each day, take every piece of paper out of your in-box and delete every e-mail in your system and repeat the previous process.

- ◆ Determine if it is dead or alive.
- ◆ Add the task to your inventory—determine what is to be done and how it is to be filed.
- ◆ Maintain priorities—new hot items always take precedence over existing warm or tepid ones.

When you practice this sunset rule everyday, you gain control of your in-box, e-mail, and paper flow. You will also discipline yourself to address tasks in their order of priority and truly maximize your effectiveness and productivity. In reality, if many of your tepid tasks are never accomplished, so be it. It is better for your career if you accomplish the really important tasks and let the minor demands take care of themselves. Most of your tepid stuff is really dead anyway. The sunset rule will help you to pull the plug appropriately!

Your real challenges are the warm tasks. The hot items are not really your problem. You have always been taking care of the hot items. It's the warm stuff that drags you down. It is not hot enough to do right away, not dead enough to throw away, so you pile it, stack it, accumulate it, and allow it to become the life giver of chaos. This system will help you to maintain control of the warm stuff and visibly demonstrate your effective organizational skills, which influence people's positive promotable perception.

The Tools of Organization

One of the advantages of today's technological explosion is the proliferation of technically advanced organizational tools. There is a wealth of software available, along with electronic organizers and traditional manual systems to help you gain better organizational control.

In utilizing any tools of organization, keep three things in mind:

1. **Find what works for you.** The scope or sophistication of the tools doesn't really matter, the important thing is the outcome of efficiency. Does it help you to exercise increased control over your time and activities, which results in higher visible productivity for you?
2. **The simpler, the better.** The more time and energy you must expend in implementing and utilizing the tool, the less likely you are to continue to use it long-term.
3. **Discipline yourself for success.** Effective organization is ingrained over an extended period of time. It becomes learned behavior. You must be willing to commit to developing your organizational skills and practicing them consistently in order to develop the habit. Organization becomes second nature if you are willing to discipline yourself for success.

Project Management Tools

There are a number of techniques typically utilized by project managers that can be helpful to you on a day-to-day basis in your quest to increase your organizational skills. Much of the software available today includes variations of these tools, or they can be implemented on paper.

Project management demands discipline and highly developed skills of organization for delivering successful outcomes within specific deadlines, and meeting quality expectations within a predetermined, acceptable range of expenses. Disorganized project managers don't survive in their professions.

Work Breakdown Structures

This effective technique is designed to take very large tasks or challenges and break them down into their smaller, manageable component parts. What may seem like an extremely complex task, too big to be achieved, looks relatively simple when broken down effectively.

Shari has been asked by the director of technical operations to research the application and possible purchase of a new gas chromatograph for the lab. This is her first opportunity to be involved in a large equipment purchase and she is very anxious to do it well. Using a work breakdown structure she created the following:

WBS (Work Breakdown Structure)
Proposal for Gas Chromatograph Purchase

#1. Analyze specs (what we want it to do and what we can afford).

1.1 Interview potential users.
1.2 Determine needs and applications.
1.2 Determine budget availability.

#2. Determine best product.

2.1 Contact manufacturer A and determine cost, availability, and spec satisfaction.
2.2 Contact manufacturer B and determine cost, availability, and spec satisfaction.
2.3 Contact manufacturer C and determine cost, availability, and spec satisfaction.
2.4 Determine ranking of available equipment options.
2.5 Arrange for demonstrations.
2.6 Contact/visit current users for observations and recommendations.

#3. Prepare proposal.
    3.1 First draft of proposal.
    3.2 Certify budget availability.
    3.3 Edit and update final proposal.

#4. Present proposal to executive committee.
    4.1 Determine best date for meeting based on attendance and availability.
    4.2 Secure conference room.
    4.3 Prepare proposal copies.
    4.4 Arrange for simultaneous product demonstrations.
    4.5 Prepare visual aids.
    4.6 Practice, practice, practice.

In this scenario, Shari breaks the overall task down into four primary activities, and further identifies these subtasks (1.1, 2.1, etc.). Highly detailed work breakdown structures actually identify sub-subtasks. This tool allows Shari to effectively plan a strategy and visually display her plan in a step-by-step, systematic format. The creation of a work breakdown structure is not done quickly or casually. (It should not be done on the back of a napkin in the restaurant where you stop for coffee on your way to work in the morning!) Taking the time to develop the foundation of a good strategy increases your chances for success.

Gantt Charts

The work breakdown structure can then be used to create a Gantt Chart, a horizontal bar chart displaying timelines and the interrelationships of the individual tasks. This very simple and highly effective tool was developed by an industrial engineer, Henry Gantt, in the early 1900s. This chart displays the time period in which a certain task is to be undertaken, identifies the sequence, and determines which tasks can be done simultaneously, and which tasks are dependent upon the previous task's completion. A Gantt Chart lists the items from the work breakdown structure down the left side of the chart and the time intervals across the top.

GANTT CHART
(Horizontal Bar Chart)
Proposal for Equipment Purchase
Week of

TASK	May 3	May 10	May 17	May 24	May 31	June 7	June 14	June 21	June 28
1. Analyze needs and specs	_____]								
2. Determine best product.				_____]					
3. Prepare proposal.						_____]			
4. Present proposal.								_____]	

The preceding illustration is a very simple example displaying only the four primary tasks from the work breakdown structure. Subtasks can also be incorporated and the Gantt Chart can be color coded to identify any delegated tasks and individual areas of responsibility. While the Gantt Chart is primarily designed as a planning tool, it can become a monitoring or reporting tool simply by color differentiation of plan *vs.* actual performance.

Analysis Charts

An additional effective project management tool is the Analysis Chart, a four-columned chart identifying potential problems and contingency plans, as the following illustration indicates.

ANALYSIS CHART

Task	What could go wrong?	Early warning sign	Contingency Plan
1. Analyze needs and specs	No product to meet specs	Comparison of specs and information from manuacturers by week of May 10	1. Reassess needs/specs to determine realistic expectations. 2. Early recommendation to delay purchase. 3. Recommendation to outsource process.
	Lack of funding	Comparison of equipment price with budget availability by May 10	1. Reassess expectations and consider less expensive equipment. 2. Research possibility of obtaining more funding. 3. Consider lease of equipment. 4. Evaluate the cost of delay of purchase and lost production. 5. Recommend no purchase or lease. 6. Recommend outsourcing.
2. Determine best product	Lack of product availability	Information from manufacturers by May 10	1. Consider second source. 2.Recommendation for short-term coverage during delay.
	Lack of available demonstration	Unable to schedule	1. Unacceptable. Delay proposal—no recommendation without demonstration.
	Poor referrals from current customers	Feedback by May 31	1. Eliminate as choice and consider another manufacturer. 2. Unacceptable, delay proposal.

ANALYSIS CHART (cont'd)

Task	What could go wrong?	Early warning sign	Contingency Plan
3. Prepare proposal	Unable to certify budget availability	Meeting with purchasing week of June 7	1. Research alternative funding. 2. Delay proposal.
4. Present proposal	Unavailability of executive committee	Personal calls to schedule date and availability week of June 7 (after budget certification)	1. Determine three alternative dates for meeting. 2. Determine those who must attend and schedule their availability only.
	Unavailability of conference/meeting room	Booking week of June 7	1. Find off-site alternative.
	Unavailability of equipment/demonstration	Discussion with manufacturer week of June 7	1. Unacceptable—red flag—reschedule.
	Equipment failure	Actual meeting mishap	1. Find back-ups for all equipment, projector, etc.

The Analysis Chart is a proactive tool, making the realistic assumption that the task will probably not go totally as planned, and encourages early consideration of contingency plans. Identifying the early warning signs is critical.

Problems identified early are always easier to fix. Problems identified late often contribute to poor quality or failure and require that someone be held accountable and blamed.

Assessing Your Organizational Skills

On a scale of 1 to 5 (1 = rarely; 5 = frequently) rate your organizational skills.

1. When someone approaches your desk or workstation, you repeat your patented phrase of, "I know this looks like a mess, but I know exactly where everything is." _____

2. Significant time is spent looking for documents or files, or asking people to provide duplicate copies of letters, documents, and the like. _____

3. Stacks of "things to do" dominate your desktop or work surfaces and expand to chairs, the floor, or other exposed areas. _____

4. You find yourself suspecting or blaming others for removing things from your desk or workspace when you cannot find what you are looking for. _____

5. Your daily plan is nonexistent or in code on the back of a napkin from McDonald's. _____

6. You have trouble determining whether something should be saved or discarded. _____

7. You find yourself under extreme time pressures and consistently have difficulty meeting deadlines. _____

8. Others find it necessary to repeatedly remind you of deadlines, or face disruptions in their work pending input or completion of work from you. _____

9. You are frequently late to meetings or forget about them. _____

10. You are frequently late in your reporting, or your reports are found to contain inaccurate or incomplete information. _____

11. Critical steps in a process are skipped or left incomplete. _____

12. Unexpected or unanticipated problems
flair up consistently. _____

Scoring:

Any score above **30** indicates a need to seek and develop organizational skill growth.

The Four Ps

*Developing your skills and demonstrating
your capabilities could be a significant
Category 2 activity for you.*

Review the prioritizing exercise presented earlier in this chapter and use it to analyze your boss's activities. Begin to identify
any of the Category 1 or 2 tasks that you may be able to assume
for him. It is an excellent opportunity to showcase yourself.

There are additional critical strategies to help you to positively impact or change how others perceive you.

Display Visible Organization

Create the vision of order, control, and efficiency. Clean up
your desk, equipment, and workspace.

*See your workspace environment through
the eyes of others.*

Snap judgments will be made concerning your organizational
skills. First impressions are lasting impressions. Keep your daily
plan and other organizational systems within reach at all times,
and avoid making notes on scraps of paper and stuffing them
in your pockets while in the view of others. When someone
asks you for something or assigns a new task, add it to your inventory of tasks, color-coded appropriately. Bring files with you

to meetings instead of loose pieces of paper. Regardless of whether or not you feel the need to make a show of organization, displaying it to others reinforces their positive perceptions.

Communicate Your Organization

Review your work breakdown structure, Gantt timeline chart, and analysis chart with your boss or anyone else who may be assisting you, providing copies when appropriate. Conduct frequent, ongoing status reviews and communicate problems or delays as soon as possible. Maximize any opportunities to communicate your situational control.

Keep Agreements

If you say you are going to do something, do it. We frequently make commitments and then get too busy to keep them or allow other priorities to impede our follow through. Enter all commitments into your inventory of tasks to utilize effective follow-up. Always be aware that others are dependent upon you for their successes. Commitments or agreements not kept may have a significant negative impact on their task. Do not develop the reputation or feed the perception that you are someone who is too disorganized to be counted on.

Practice Prompt Responses

Respond to requests and messages as promptly as possible. Carefully monitor e-mail and voice mail messages, seizing opportunities to impress others with your quick response. Use Do Not Disturb or any phone management systems carefully. Consistently being unavailable may send a message of being overwhelmed by your current workload. Others may be waiting for your response before they can proceed, and the slightest delay on your part not only slows them down, it also makes you a target to be blamed. Repeated claims that you never got back to someone, never responded, or were unavailable will have a significant negative impact on the perceptions of others, and decrease your promotability.

Every time you hear comments like, "Wow, that was fast," or "You really turned that around quickly," your promotability quotient moves up a notch.

Organize Your Reading to Stay Abreast of Current Economic and Industry Developments

While it is impossible to read all of the relevant material or publications affecting your industry or job, it is important to identify at least a few critical resources and read, review, and route them.

Read the business sections in your hometown newspaper, *USA Today,* and one other major, nationally recognized publication (*New York Times, Washington Post, Wall Street Journal,* etc.) every day. Also review a minimum of one business publication per month (*Fortune, Forbes, Business Weekly,* etc.), along with a minimum of one industry or technology-related publication (trade magazine, etc.). If you belong to any professional organizations, read their monthly publications and mailings. Quickly review the table of contents or article headlines and tear out any information that appears interesting or relevant. Carry it with you in a current reading file (do not carry the entire magazine or newspaper) and use any short opportunities to read (lunch, waiting to meet with someone, the doctor's office, airplane, etc.).

Any relevant information interesting to you, your boss and other promotion decision makers or influencers should be copied and routed or faxed with a note, "I found this to be interesting, and thought you might enjoy it. Let me know what you think."

Read at least four organizational skill development books per year and use any opportunities to reference this material in discussions, memos, or reports. When you attend training sessions, always write a summary of what you learned, how you can use it effectively, and distribute this as broadly as possible.

Preempt Time Deadlines

If someone is expecting something from you on the fourth of the month, make sure they receive it on the third. This pertains especially to your reporting. *Never* be late with your reports. Try to be the first in and avoid being the last at all costs. If your boss finds it necessary to repeatedly remind you of late reports or missed deadlines, it will have a lasting negative impact on your potential promotability.

An effective tool in deadline management is the utilization of an efficient tickler file. This may be a series of computer prompts built into your software or the mere maintenance of manual expandable files with separately marked tabs (one for each day of the month).

 The key to deadline management is "tickle yourself early."

Help Others Meet Their Critical Deadlines

Discover the deadlines of others: your direct boss, key promotion decision makers and any other influencers, and significant peers. Communicate your awareness of their time requirements and your willingness to help them. Referencing their pending deadlines helps to reinforce their awareness and always impresses them with your thoroughness. Inquiries such as, "I know the proposal is due in two weeks. Is there anything I can do to help you meet that deadline?" are very powerful. You may also try offering proactive suggestions, such as: "I know the proposal is due in two weeks. Would it be helpful to you if I did this

. . . or if I developed this information?" Demonstrating to others your awareness of the demands and pressures on them, and your willingness to help them be successful can be very impressive.

Exceed Expectations Whenever Possible

Meeting the expectations of others is necessary in today's workplace, but it probably won't get you promoted. Exceeding their expectations will. Not only is it essential to exceed time expectations, but also quality expectations. When someone asks you for information, provide it accurately and in a form ready-made for distribution and use. If someone asks you for last year's figures, provide a comparison for the last five years also. These are additional opportunities to visibly demonstrate your efficiency and organization. Keep challenging yourself. What else can you provide or do that would be helpful? Even if your additional efforts are not particularly helpful, you have made an impression by your willingness to go the extra mile. Exceeding expectations also allows you to informally accumulate IOUs or favors to be called in at a later date. Accumulating this wealth of good will can be invaluable.

Beware of Budget Constraints

Regardless of what you are doing, budget or cost is an issue. There is always a fine line between time, quality, and dollar considerations on which you must balance. As mentioned earlier regarding workplace realities, always be a prudent watchdog concerning expenses. Avoid the extreme perceptions of being seen as either too cheap or too extravagant, and always ask yourself, "Is there a less expensive or more efficient way of accomplishing this same outcome?" Continually search for better ways of reducing costs internally while avoiding any reduction of spending that impacts the organization externally (in the view of customers, clients, patients, students, the press, or the greater community at large).

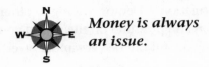

*Money is always
an issue.*

Real-World Promotion Mentoring

Oliver Jordan is the Affirmative Action and Training Manager at the Pennsylvania Convention Center in Philadelphia. The Convention Center opened in June of 1993 and has become one of the fastest growing facilities of its type on the East Coast. Oliver offered as a typical example of successful promotability, the following:

> *We have hired a number of people as administrative assistants whose intentions were not to remain in these jobs for a long period of time, but to be promoted to Event Coordinators or perhaps leadership positions in the Facility Services or Exhibitor Services departments. To demonstrate their abilities and willingness to be promoted, one of the things they frequently asked to do was to assist in working special events, even to the extent of asking to shadow an Event Coordinator or someone in the Exhibitor Services department. They would observe firsthand how these departments were organized and what the jobs entail. These departments are responsible for planning events, customer satisfaction, and providing our clients with the specific tools they need in terms of their exhibition booths and space. The Convention Center has been unique in the sense that whenever anyone has shown an interest in moving to another department, we have been more than flexible and willing to give them the opportunity to do so. We are developing a cross-training program for our entire staff to help people learn additional skills.*

> *Organizational skills are critical. Part of that is effective follow-up. You have got to be detailed and as oftentime said, "the devil is in the details." But in our business, it is critical to follow-up because customer service is our lifeline. You have to have the capacity to be*

organized, you have got to be detailed, and you must also be flexible. That is so much a key to promotability. In this business, an event can change, you may have more attendees than planned, or circumstances can change, the electricity could go out at any moment, and you have to be organized enough to accommodate any and all possibilities.

What does Oliver Jordan recommend to you in navigating your next promotion?

You have to make your promotion goals known, be willing to extend yourself to earn the promotion, and you've got to have the organizational skills that are going to allow you to survive in a really fast-paced environment.

SIX

RISK TAKING, PROBLEM SOLVING, DECISION MAKING

The pursuit of promotion demands a willingness to take appropriate risks. This is a far different scenario from the historical or traditional strategy of playing it safe, sitting back, keeping your nose clean, staying out of trouble, and waiting for longevity to dictate promotion.

 In the past, inaction was your ally, today inaction is your enemy.

Colossal failure can do serious harm to your promotability, especially for those who are already in the upper echelon of the organization. A huge, highly visible mishandling of a situation can permanently stall your career (although not always!). However, for those seeking to jump-start or accelerate their career growth, seizing the opportunity to successfully embrace risk and excel where others choose to play it safe can boost your promotability. You must be willing to take risks, and doing so successfully allows you to catapult over your internal competition.

This chapter helps you to sharpen your SAW by offering tools for assessing risks, solving problems, and implementing effective decisions.

Risk Taking

The important thing is to assess the risk effectively and develop a strategy for success. Risk taking, problem solving, and decision making are intertwined. Risk taking can be defined as the willingness to confront problems or anticipate opportunities and make decisions, recommend appropriate actions or solutions, and take responsibility for the ultimate outcomes. Many people are willing to think through problems and make recommendations to others, which is a reasonably safe, risk-free strategy, however, you, as the decisive promotion seeker, must be willing to move from thought and recommendation to action and accountability. Even those who risk and err increase their visibility and gain respect from others by their mere willingness to take the initiative. Risk takers are admired, and while many profess to be willing, few actually make the journey. Some lie in wait, ready to pounce, ridicule, and harshly judge any risk takers who stumble. Unfortunately, they are probably the ones destined to remain in the lower regions of the organizational food chain, entrenched by their own limitations.

First, you must develop the positive risk taking, problem solving mindset.

◆ **Assume success.** If you doubt your abilities, your lack of confidence will be glaringly obvious to others. If you're not sure you can solve the problem—you're right—you probably can't. If you don't believe you can do it, don't take the risk. You may also want to rethink your pursuit of promotion. Why should people be promoted who don't believe they can make positive things happen?

◆ **Realize that "challenges and risks" may be your fast-track tickets to stardom.** The challenge of tackling a problem head-on and generating a successful resolution is a golden opportunity to display your talents and promotability. Careers have been successfully established by decisively reacting to problems and proving the ability to perform well under stress, pressure, and during crises. When you become known throughout the organization as someone always ready to tackle the tough tasks and tame the problems others shrink from, your promotability skyrockets. Do not dread or avoid problems, they are valuable opportunities to make a contribution and market your abilities.

◆ **Depersonalize failure.** Successfully dealing with risks and solving problems contributes to your promotability. Do not fall into the trap of perceiving that a lack of success devalues you or indicates incompetence. If it doesn't go well, some *thing* went wrong. Identify that *thing*. Learn from it and succeed at your next challenge. Failure isn't personal.

The two primary aspects of risk taking are assessing how appropriate the risk is and determining the most effective action.

Assess the Appropriateness of the Risk

◆ What is the challenge? Clearly identify the problem or the opportunity.

◆ What is the potential upside to be gained? Will a positive outcome enhance your promotability? (This determines whether the risk is worth it.)

◆ What is the possible downside? Would a worst-case scenario have a significant negative impact on your current or future promotability? How much risk are you comfortable with? Would a lack of success be a permanent hindrance or a bump in the road?

◆ How will you know if the risk starts to go bad? Will you be able to identify problems early enough to prevent significant career-damaging failure?

◆ How will you handle a potentially negative outcome? What is your contingency plan if the risk-taking opportunity isn't successful?

The more risk averse you are, the lower your promotability.

Discretion is the better part of valor, and knowing the point at which a risk becomes too great is a valuable asset, however, the closer you are willing to approach that line, the greater the opportunity you have to score a highly visible, promotion-impacting victory.

As a general guideline, the greater the potential for positive payoff and the higher your level of confidence in creating a positive outcome, the more personal responsibility you want to accept for any risks. The less acceptable the risk and the lower your level of confidence in creating a positive outcome, the more you want to broaden the responsibility and invite others into the decision-making process. If the risk is too great, spread the accountability for negative fallout.

Determine the Most Effective Action

Patterns of indecision, inaction, or unwillingness to intervene in the face of problems, hurt your career. When facing a choice, you are much better off committing errors of *commission* (doing something!), rather than omission (doing nothing!). Errors of commission (taking the wrong action or making a mistake) can frequently be fixed. Errors of omission (not taking action when it is demanded) can rarely be corrected, and it is usually impossible to reclaim the opportunity for correction. Once it's gone, it's gone forever.

Problem Solving and Effective Decision Making

Any effective problem-solving and decision-making process has three critical parts:

1. Identification of the problem or challenge
2. Diagnosis of the root cause or critical factors
3. Creation of appropriate solutions

Of these three critical parts, identification is the easiest; diagnosis is the most critical and the least practiced; and successful solutions are usually obvious. When proper diagnosis is accomplished, the success of the ultimate outcome depends greatly on the depth and effectiveness of this diagnosis.

It takes little talent to identify the existence of a problem. The most negative, unpromotable dregs of the organization are extremely skilled at merely identifying problems. They are very quick to point out what's wrong and who's to blame. The real challenge is to diagnose the problem and identify appropriate, realistic, and effective solutions. Your display of effective diagnostic abilities will greatly increase your organizational value and promotability. When diagnosis is incomplete, you leap from identification directly to solution, resulting in the treatment of symptoms, not root causes. This perpetuates making the same mistakes over and over.

Case Study Example

A service organization began to experience a troubling increase in its accounts receivable collection cycle. Previously, they averaged payments from their clients thirty-three days after the service was provided. Rather quickly, this lengthened to thirty-eight days and showed signs of continuing erosion. Obviously, this caused major concern, disruption of cash flow, and predictable internal problems. The initial response was to increase the pressure on the accounts receivable department, which resulted in more aggressive collection tactics, with corresponding increases in client complaints and dissatisfaction. Offended by the new, more aggressive policies, some clients severed their service agreements. When the organization finally took the time to diagnose the actual problem, they discovered that an internal problem in the billing process was actually delaying the original invoicing by three to five days. In reality, the collection cycle really hadn't changed. Clients were still paying in the same amount of time, but the organization was experiencing an unrecognized delay in the initial billing procedure. This wasn't a collection problem, it was a billing problem. Therefore, the initial lack of diagnosis resulted in attempts to fix the wrong process and an unacceptable alienation of valuable clients. The person who ultimately diagnosed and corrected the problem successfully certainly increased his visibility and promotability.

The three problem-solving/decision-making steps are sequential.

Identification

Successful identification is accurately qualifying results and observations. It is important to be as detailed and as factual as possible, emphasizing objectivity over subjectivity. Be wary of opinions that are stated as, or perceived to be, facts. Separate fact from opinion, and emotion from reality. It is of paramount importance to depersonalize issues. Identify *what* is happening, not *who* is doing it.

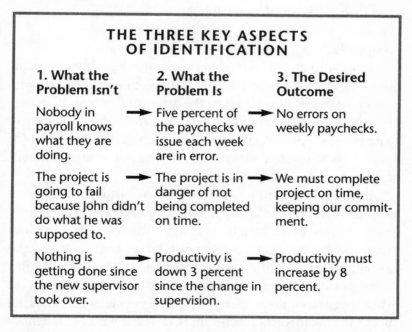

THE THREE KEY ASPECTS OF IDENTIFICATION		
1. What the Problem Isn't	**2. What the Problem Is**	**3. The Desired Outcome**
Nobody in payroll knows what they are doing. ➝	Five percent of the paychecks we issue each week are in error. ➝	No errors on weekly paychecks.
The project is going to fail because John didn't do what he was supposed to. ➝	The project is in danger of not being completed on time. ➝	We must complete project on time, keeping our commitment.
Nothing is getting done since the new supervisor took over. ➝	Productivity is down 3 percent since the change in supervision. ➝	Productivity must increase by 8 percent.

Once these three factors have been identified, consider the impact and determine the value to you and the organization of correcting the situation. To determine if the problem is really worth the investment of time, effort, and resources, you must ask yourself:

1. Is this really a problem?
2. So what? (Does it matter?)
3. Does anybody else care or is it my issue only?
4. What is to be gained by fixing it?
5. Does it impact our efficiency? Promotability? Customer service?
6. Will championing this issue increase my promotability?
7. Should I address this unilaterally or in a collaborative effort with others?

If you're the only one who thinks it's a problem and no one else cares, don't invest your time. However, if the answers to these questions are favorable, then thoroughly assess the risk and proceed through the problem-solving process.

Diagnosis

The key to diagnosis is addressing *why* the problem is occurring. You cannot effectively solve a problem until you know its exact root cause. Paramount in the diagnostic process is gathering the relevant information and knowing what to look for. Doing this is a critical, often overlooked step. The penchant for taking quick, decisive action and making something happen, frequently causes this step to be disregarded.

Improper diagnosis often degenerates into an impulsive reaction of blaming and scapegoating. Are people ever the problem? Sure. However, by a huge margin, the source of the problem is probably caused by elements other than human (the actual process, lack of resources, equipment, barriers to performance, etc.). Solutions are usually simple and straightforward when diagnosis is done effectively. Many people believe that the most valuable medical practitioners are those who can diagnose what's actually wrong, not necessarily those who recommend appropriate therapies. You cannot determine the appropriate corrective action for solving a problem until you have accurately diagnosed its source.

There are a number of tools to assist you in this diagnostic process. The best way to begin is to ask the compelling questions: Why aren't we already achieving our desired outcome? What is causing the problem to occur? And why haven't we already solved the problem? These questions are designed to encourage you to look at the root causes. The more accurate your look, the more success you will have.

Penetrate Five Depths of the Cause

It is important to ask *why* at least five times in order to eliminate the temptation of jumping from identification to solution. For example, in a manufacturing plant, a production line routinely blows fuses. Typically this is diagnosed as a fuse problem and the solution is to replace the fuse and restart the line.

The five-depths process asks the following questions.

Question	Answer
1. What makes the production line stop?	"We blow fuses."
2. What makes the fuses blow?	"The generator slips."
3. What makes the generator slip?	"It isn't receiving proper lubrication."
4. Why isn't the generator receiving proper lubrication?	"The automated lubrication tool is clogged with lint."
5. What causes the lubrication tool to be clogged with lint?	"The filter is improperly placed or somehow damaged, allowing airborne lint and debris to accumulate."

Is this really a fuse problem? Obviously not, it is a filter problem. The appropriate solution is to clean the lubricating tool, fix and/or replace the filter, and *then* change the fuse. Unfortunately, the typical reaction would be to continually replace fuses until the generator fatally malfunctions, resulting in a crisis (production loss and unnecessary costs due to downtime, emergency generator replacement, etc.).

Visibly Display the Problem

Put the problem on paper. A flowchart or a process diagram will help you to *see* the root cause. For example, Rob is in the shipping department. He is concerned with the frequent criticism the department receives because customers are not getting their deliveries in a timely manner. The shipping department feels the order processing department is actually to blame. But they are denying any accountability by saying they are doing the best they can and the customers just have to put up with any occasional delivery problems. Unsatisfied, Rob meets with Diane, the order processing supervisor. They take a roll of paper and stretch it across a desk. With color-coded Post-it notes, they identify each specific step in the combined order processing/ shipping processes. Decision or action points are coded and several clear "aha's" become evident. They realize a bottleneck is being created because all orders have to be approved by one specific person prior to being released to the shipping department. When this person is absent, in a meeting, or swamped with other tasks, the orders are delayed. Rob and Diane then begin to analyze alternative methods of obtaining order approval. However, until they actually saw the problem on paper, the root cause could not easily be identified.

Assess Resources and Barriers

Is a lack of available resources at the root of the problem? Are there barriers, real or imagined, that are causing or contributing to the problem? (In the previous example, the shipping problem was actually a barrier in the order process that created a bottleneck.)

The following are some items you should consider.

Resources	Barriers
Materials	Physical alignment
Manpower	Technology
Equipment	Organizational cultures
Time	Training
Dollars	Methods
	Policies
	Procedures

If the root cause of the problem involves a resource or barrier issue, the question, "How can we obtain the necessary resources or remove the existing barriers?" must be answered.

 If the resource or barrier issues cannot be successfully addressed, the problem will not be solved.

Determine the Pervasiveness of the Problem

Key questions: Is the problem an isolated incident? Where else is it happening? Who else is having the problem? Is this similar to anything we have experienced in the past?

Answering these questions effectively will help to define the scope of your diagnosis. If the problem is systemwide, or pervasive throughout the organization, there may not be a local cause or easily implemented solution. (This would, however, be a great opportunity to lead a cross-functional, broad-based, problem-solving effort). If effective solutions to similar problems have been found in the past, it would be advantageous to discover the details of the previous diagnoses and solutions.

Creation of Appropriate Solutions

Solutions are the desired result of any problem-solving challenge. Frequently, to the "solver goes the spoils" (rewards, recognition, visibility, etc.).

Any solutions must be consistent with the objectives, policies, and culture of the organization, department, or customer. They must always realistically consider the costs in dollars, effort, and time. Solutions must also incorporate monitoring provisions to insure continued success and quick identification of any emerging problems.

When creating solutions, begin by considering a minimum of three alternatives. It is extremely important to broaden or expand the number of possibilities and avoid narrowing your options too quickly. To determine a minimum of three possible alternatives, you may have to consider fifteen! However, through the process of elimination, you will narrow your options down from the plausible many to the realistic few. Here are some tools you should employ in the process.

Assess the Availability of Resources

What resources are actually available to help solve the problem? Two key considerations: Are the resources available? Can you acquire them? You must realistically consider competition from others, current and future organizational priorities, and so on. While there may currently be enough dollars available to fund your solution, others may be competing for these same dollars and command a claim of higher urgency or priority. Also, consider how you will obtain the necessary resources. What is your strategy? Who can help you acquire them? What will it cost you in the long term? What will you have to give up in the future to acquire these resources today, and is it worth it?

In considering your solution alternatives, you must ask the questions: Can I utilize more people? Invest more hours in the task or project? Spend more money?

Assess the Barriers

Are there barriers hindering the resolution of the problem? If so, can you remove these barriers, and how will you do it?

When considering your solution alternatives, be sure to ask

yourself: Can I change the process? Adjust policies and procedures? Rearrange physical alignments? Upgrade or adjust technology? Change the organizational culture or perception?

Solutions to Similar Problems

Have similar problems occurred in the past within the organization? Do you know people outside your organization who may have experienced something similar? What can you learn from their experiences? What did they do well? What did they try that didn't work? Can you avoid reinventing the wheel by capitalizing on the valuable experiences of others? Discuss what they would do differently if they were faced with the same problem again. It is critical to guard against perceiving the input of others to be detrimental. Do not be threatened by their experience.

Seeking the advice or counsel of others is not a sign of weakness, it is a sign of maturity and efficiency.

Learn from the mistakes and actions of others. (*Please note*: If others are helpful to you by sharing insights, ideas, or past experiences, be sure to appropriately thank, credit, and acknowledge them.)

Use Personal or Interactive Brainstorming

Brainstorming is an exceptionally effective solution-generating tool. The goal of a brainstorming session is to generate a quantity of ideas, not necessarily quality ones— and to uncover potential initial options without any discussion of their merits or details.

Personal brainstorming sessions require merely sitting down in a quiet setting, allowing a specific period of uninterrupted time (twenty minutes is probably optimum), and listing as many alternatives as you can possibly think of. Remember, it isn't necessary to consider: how you would make them happen, their relationship to other options, or the negative or positive consequences.

A self-imposed time limit creates urgency, and such deadlines drive performance! Also, keep a legal pad or microcassette recorder close by at all times. (You may get your best ideas when you are standing in the shower.)

Interactive brainstorming sessions involving others are extremely helpful and can be fun as well as highly productive. Establish a time limit (again, twenty minutes), frame a topic for discussion (How can we solve this production problem?), and encourage the generation of as many ideas as possible. There are two formats that can be adapted for interactive brainstorming sessions, formal and informal brainstorming.

Formal brainstorming allows participants to voice their ideas in a predetermined order, providing as many ideas as possible during the allotted time. Only one person speaks at a time and individuals are permitted to pass occasionally when it's their turn, however, no one is permitted to pass two times in succession. There is no commentary or rejection of anyone's contribution and there is no such thing as a bad idea. Allowing any demonstrations of rejection, either verbal or nonverbal, instantaneously destroys a brainstorming session. When the allotted time is up, a discussion of merits will begin to reveal any unusable or unrealistic ideas. By generating a wealth of options, it is likely that high quality alternatives will be in there somewhere.

For informal brainstorming, present a topic, establish a time limit, and allow everyone to participate in a free-for-all discussion. These sessions are usually less productive. Typically, you end up hearing the same ideas from the same dominant people, while the quiet ones choose not to involve themselves. In general, formally structured brainstorming sessions yield much greater results.

A variation of brainstorming utilizes a two-phase process of planning and presentation.

◆ **Planning.** Present your topic to a group (How can we solve this production problem?) and give the participants a short period of time to quietly gather their thoughts and ideas. Have them create a short outline of their thoughts and recommendations. Three to five minutes is usually sufficient, though the allotted time for this planning activity is not cast in stone. It is better to err on the side of too little time than too much. This structured planning period provides an opportunity to gather one's thoughts and prepare for participation prior to the actual discussion.

◆ **Presentation.** In a predetermined order, participants are given a specific period of time to present their ideas to the group with no discussion, questions, or interruptions from the others. These presentations are carefully timed. A timekeeper is appointed and no one is allowed to exceed the allotted time (two to three minutes is a guideline). It is extremely important to predetermine the presentation order to insure equal and total participation. It is also wise to position any leaders (formal or informal) toward the latter part of the rotation to insure that their ideas do not dominate or influence other presentations. If their ideas are introduced first, others will frequently form positions of total support or predictable opposition to their presentations and the process will become distorted.

When the presentation phase is over, the ideas are prioritized, grouped together by common factors, and discussed for effectiveness and realism. Discussions do not begin until all of the ideas have surfaced equally.

This planning and presentation technique differs from traditional brainstorming because it allows each participant to explain their recommendation in depth.

Develop Realistic, Appropriate Solutions

In the decision distillation process, the required three options that emerge must be based in real-world, acceptable, and appropriate terms. Problem solving is not the time to get bogged down in playing "If only we had . . . " Lamenting what you do not have is counterproductive and doesn't result in correction. Problem solving must be anchored in reality and consistent with the existing organizational culture, financial circumstance, and a realistic assessment of resources and barriers. The greater the crisis, problem, or challenge, the more damaging and unproductive it is to lament.

Problem solutions can be structured around the components of time, expense, and quality of performance. Chart your options as the following example illustrates.

SOLUTION OPTION CHART

Time	Expense
Which realistic solution provides the quickest fix?	Which realistic solution incurs the least cost?
Which realistic solution takes longest to implement?	Which realistic solution incurs the most cost?
Which realistic solution falls in between the quickest and the longest?	Which realistic solution falls in between least and most?

Quality of Performance

Which realistic solution meets the bare minimum standards of quality?

Which realistic solution meets or exceeds exceptional quality performance?

Which realistic solution falls between the minimum and high range of quality performance?

This format applies the individual components of time, expense, and quality of performance to the structure of good, better, or best options. Once these are established, decide which component is most critical or dominant. Is it time (it must be done quickly)? Expense (it must be done as cheaply as possible)? Quality of performance (only exceptional quality is acceptable)? Once the dominant component is identified, the process of elimination begins.

Always be aware that while one component may dominate, the other two will have some measure of influence, and though the importance may vary, expense is always an issue.

Determine the Optimum Solution

This is where the problem-solving challenge intensifies in risk, and provides a great opportunity to distance yourself from the crowd. At this point you will either announce your decision and begin to take the necessary action if you are empowered to do so, or you will pass your recommendations on to the appropriate decision makers.

Once you have determined your optimum solution, consider these factors:

◆ **Trial balloons.** Before you commit to a recommendation or take action, consider all other individuals or areas (departments, teams, facilities) that will be impacted. Be aware of the ripple effect. Any action you either take or recommend will have an impact on others. Anyone who may be even remotely affected should be notified of your recommendations or plans prior to implementation. This is a great "what if . . . " opportunity.

"One of the things I'm considering in dealing with this problem is . . . Does this sound like a reasonable solution to you and how will it affect you or your department?" Raising the awareness of others prior to the actual decision or recommendation gains valuable input and increases their chances of support.

Many people react negatively to "surprises" discovered after the fact.

◆ **Experimentation.** If at all possible, your solution should contain a plan for limited experimentation. Try it in one limited area and monitor the impact. Experimentation makes it easier for others to lend support and provides the opportunity for some assessment and adjustment before any formal commitment to total action is made. While experimentation may not always be appropriate, utilize the strategy whenever possible.

Always be the one to perform, guide, or lead the experimentation.

Track Your Optimum Solution

Your solution must address the following critical factors:

◆ Who is going to do it?
◆ What are they going to do?
◆ When will it be accomplished?
◆ How will we know it's done?
◆ How will success or failure be measured?

Problem-Solving and Decision-Making Assessment

	Yes	No
1. Have I clearly defined the problem we are experiencing?	☐	☐
2. Have I identified the desired outcome?	☐	☐
3. Have I correctly diagnosed the root cause of the problem?	☐	☐
4. Have I assessed the contributions, potential, and/or constraints of barriers and resources?	☐	☐
5. Have I considered all reasonable alternative solutions?	☐	☐

	Yes	No
6. Have I effectively prioritized the criticality of time, expenses, and quality of performance?	☐	☐
7. Have I surfaced the most attractive option?	☐	☐
8. Have I clearly differentiated:		
Who?	☐	☐
What?	☐	☐
When?	☐	☐
How will we know?	☐	☐
9. Have I structured effective early warning signs and appropriate contingency plans for potential problems?	☐	☐
10. Have I communicated in a clear, concise manner:		
The problem?	☐	☐
The cause?	☐	☐
The desired outcome?	☐	☐
The alternatives?	☐	☐
The recommendation?	☐	☐
Potential setbacks?	☐	☐
Contingency plans?	☐	☐

Your candor in completing this assessment is extremely important. Any *no* responses should be reviewed and addressed. Self-serving or inappropriate *yes* responses can be deadly. The result will be flawed problem solving and decision making, which will increase the risk of promotion-killing mistakes.

The Four Ps

Henry Ford is believed to have said, "Failure is nothing more than an opportunity to begin again more knowledgeably." When you consider that life is a series of opportunities to fail your way to success, failure begins to look more attractive. The key to failure is managing the risk and demonstrating the learning that results from the failure. Those who don't learn from their failures resemble a hamster on its wheel, exerting lots of energy but going nowhere.

Be Willing to Fail

Be discerning in prioritizing your challenges. Do not become a missionary in search of lost causes. On the other hand, do not fall into the trap of safety either. Identify high-profile challenges that have a reasonable chance of success and be willing to commit yourself to action. Playing it safe gets you nowhere.

Don Quixote was an inspirational character, but he never got promoted.

Demonstrate Persistence in Problem Solving

If your initial attempt at addressing a challenge is unsuccessful, don't fold up your tent and go home. That's easy, and takes no talent. Persistence is a key to promotability. As previously mentioned, the important thing is to analyze your lack of success, learn from the mistakes, and formulate a different plan of attack. Only dummies continue to make the same mistakes over and over again. The people earning promotions are those who correctly analyze, diagnose, regroup, reformulate, and implement new plans and midcourse corrections.

Lack of persistence is a promotion knockout.

Break Through the Constrained Thinking of Traditional Problem Solving

Overcome the limitations of experience, education, training, beliefs, and "the way things have always been done around here." Seek input from others who can "see the forest for the trees" and view problems from as many perspectives as possible.

(Approach shipping problems as if you were the box being shipped.) Analyze the challenge from the customer's point of view, and the perspective of *all* internal personnel, teams, departments, or groups that may have any involvement in the process. For example, to determine the best way to stop flooding from occurring, ask yourself, "What would the water do?" and factor that perspective into your plan.

Problem solving also means change—doing things differently. Avoid the perception that you see change as a threat. To improve is to change. Your promotability depends on your willingness to change often. Seize every opportunity to enhance being perceived as an agent of change.

Actively Support Others in Their Problem-Solving Efforts

Position yourself as a problem-solving resource to others. Willingly share your creativity, experiences, and insights. Your own problem-solving efforts will be enhanced through involvement with others as you learn from their successes and failures. Long term, others will perceive you as a capable and willing resource. You can cultivate valuable allies in your quest for promotion by helping others achieve. Withholding support is actually seen as "subtle sabotage" and can result in permanent barriers to promotability.

Never withhold your support of others. If you can help them to be successful, do so.

Always Offer Solutions in Tandem with Problems

Identifying problems alone is a negative activity. Offering possible solutions to problems is proactive. If you don't have a solution to a problem, clearly establish your willingness to embrace responsibility for the ultimate outcome. "This is the problem, and while I don't yet have the solution, I would like to take responsibility for finding an answer. I will create a cross-functional problem-solving team, or I will research what we have done in the past and also develop some creative new ways to deal with this problem . . . " Seize every opportunity to imbed in the brains of your boss and other promotion decision makers and influencers, the perception of you as a valuable employee who realistically anticipates and assesses problems and offers appropriate, reasonable solutions.

Playing "Chicken Little" by telling everyone the sky is falling won't get you promoted. Figuring out what to do about the falling sky will!

Effectively Deal with the "Trolls on the Highway of Life"

The trolls on the highway of life are those people who lie in wait, coiled to pounce on any new idea or proposal for change. Their mantras are:

- ◆ "We've been doing it this way for fifteen years, no reason to change now."
- ◆ "We tried that once. Didn't work then, won't work now."
- ◆ "That idea will never work."
- ◆ "That may have worked somewhere else, but it won't work here."

Trolls, although nauseating creatures, are a fact of life. Deal with them effectively and move on. The formula for troll management is:

◆ **Listen.** As distasteful as trolls are, the truth is, they may have some accurate observations. While they want their observations to be the basis for inaction, you can use their observations as the basis for contingency plans for insuring their predictions do not occur.

◆ **Acknowledge their observations.** "That's an interesting observation. I can see how you might feel that way. I'm sure your perceptions are based on experience."

◆ **Brainstorm options.** "How *can* we make it work this

time? What can we do to insure your feared problems don't occur? What can we do to make sure we're successful?"

◆ **Walk away.** Don't let the trolls take you down. They are yappy little creatures, nipping at your ankles. Deflect them and move on.

Consistently Depersonalize Problems

The tendency of many organizations and individuals is to quickly identify the villain when problems occur. Let's find somebody to blame, hang him out to dry, and deflect any responsibility from ourselves. Always be the person to say, "Let's get away from personalities and look at issues. Let's talk about *what* happened, not *who* did it. Let's talk about how to fix problems, not who to blame. If it's necessary to assign negative responsibility to someone, there will be plenty of time for that later." People who are quick to blame others erode their base of allies and few people want to collaborate with them. Trust evaporates at warp speed.

Become Anticipatory

No plan, project, or endeavor of any kind goes totally as planned. Things go wrong. It's a fact of life. Be anticipatory. Try to anticipate where potential breakdowns might happen. Plan reasonable, appropriate responses and monitor vigilantly. Expect probable, positive outcomes, but acknowledge possible downsides and don't let them catch you off guard. The important thing once again is to have contingency plans. The Chicken Littles of the organization run around telling everybody that the sky is falling; your role is knowing where to find the umbrellas! To be anticipatory is to be vigilant.

A wise old gambler once said, "Trust everyone and cut the cards." A mideastern rephrasing of this same sentiment is, "Trust Allah *and* tie up your camel." Well-thought-out contingency plans serve you well. The best friend you may ever have is the contingency plan that you don't have to use.

Avoid Turf Battles

In today's interactive collaborative environment, marking off your territory and defending it against intrusion is both unproductive and career damaging. Your focus is not defending your turf, your focus is contributing to overall organizational productivity. Your turf is the entire organization— anywhere you can apply your skills, abilities, and willingness. Allowing others to have input and influence in your areas of responsibility enhances creativity, drives your learning process, and results in higher productivity for all. Nothing is more unbecoming than the snarling beast defending his barren territory while the land all around him is brimming with lush growth and vegetation. Erect no barbed wire!

Maintain Calm and Focus Under Pressure

Problem solving frequently takes place in high-stress, high-pressure crisis circumstances. This is a tremendous opportunity to demonstrate your control under pressure and ability to function successfully when others may be imploding from the pressure. Crises are highly visible opportunities to display your superstar ability. Escalating conflict, spreading negativity, or abusive verbal or behavioral displays are signs of folding under pressure.

Embrace Responsibility

If a problem is yours, own it. Running for cover and deflecting responsibility may have short-term appeal, however, in the long term, it can damage your eligibility for promotion. Because it happens so infrequently in today's workplace, people who step up and take responsibility are like an oasis in the desert. Your message should be: "Here's what happened . . . I take total responsibility. Here's what was learned . . . Here's how we will avoid this problem in the future . . . Here's what we will do to fix the problem now . . ."

Also, avoid extended apologies, groveling, or dramatic mea culpas. Maturely take responsibility, put it behind you, and move on. While problems may damage career growth, squarely facing responsibility and willingly facing accountability enhance it.

Real-World Promotion Mentoring

David Tate is the Executive Vice President of East Manufacturing Co. in Randolph, Ohio. East Manufacturing is one of the top twenty tractor trailer manufacturers in the United States. They employ a workforce of 475 people, manufacturing specialized aluminum dump trailers, flatbed trailers, refuse trailers, and related aftermarket accessories. David is a 1967 graduate of the United States Naval Academy and served as an officer in the U.S. Navy for six years prior to entering civilian life.

David said that what he looks for in promotable employees is their character base. He holds integrity in high regard:

> *I look for integrity. Do they do what they say they're going to do and can I count on them to tell me the truth, whether they think I'm going to like it or not? Integrity is not telling somebody something you think they want to hear. I also look for a strong goal system. I believe one's ability to get organized and plan and look to the future begins with their goal system. This includes life goals and job goals, and how one can balance the demands of the various goal areas. People can have minimal direction and still maintain high initiative on a daily basis if they have their goal system established. I also want to know how well they deal with adversity and criticism. Do they rebound well from a setback, and are they coachable? Do they have the ability to objectively look at themselves and say, "I'm willing to accept critical feedback for the purpose of improving"? Promotable employees are "givers," with a sincere desire to contribute to the organization and improve the company. I also want to know how objective they are in terms of accepting and taking responsibility for their actions. Do they make excuses when problems arise, or do they willingly take responsibility for unsuccessful results?*

When asked what he would recommend as a mentor to

those seeking promotion, David said:

> *The first thing would be to assess the skills necessary for the job into which you want to be promoted. A person has to look at himself and say, "Does that job tie into my strengths or is it drawing from my weaknesses? Do I have the skill sets to meet the requirements of that job?" Secondly, it's important to show that you're trying to gain the skills, knowledge, and education necessary to do that job successfully. Achieving excellence in your current job and demonstrating a desire to make a difference for the benefit of the company are obvious factors which will affect your promotion opportunities.*

David also expressed the importance of exhibiting leadership.

> *Leadership skills, regardless of your position in the organization, can set you apart from others. You don't need a group of people reporting to you to demonstrate leadership. The traits and skills of successful leaders, such as encouraging people and making them feel good about what they're doing, promoting teamwork and collaboration, or giving your best effort at your job and setting a good example, are all indications of leadership potential. Employees who display the attitude and characteristics of a leader regardless of their position can have a tremendously positive effect on the organization. This includes being a creative problem solver, making decisions from a position of confidence and doing what is best for the organization, not for one's individual needs. I believe a major challenge in our company is to improve the leadership of middle managers. We need to take them from the constraints of their job function to ownership beyond their specific area, thinking more from a company perspective. They must realize that they can have a tremendous influence on other people in cross-functional areas of the company if they think and act as a person trying to make a difference.*

David certainly believes that displaying leadership and effective, broad-based decision making is essential to being promoted. He also stresses the importance of demonstrating a willingness to help the organization grow. Taking initiative is critical.

SEVEN

ESTABLISHING EFFECTIVE WORKPLACE RELATIONSHIPS

Developing people skills—the ability to interact productively with others building successful workplace relationships—is a critical component of your promotability. Some individuals are instinctively "people persons," others must work diligently at building their skills, though we all must strive to increase our ability to work with others.

There are many significant relationship destroyers, but this chapter will help you to sharpen your relationship-building SAW and avoid the potential damage that can be done to your career.

Factors that destroy internal relationships may be:

- ◆ Unmet expectations
- ◆ Resentment
- ◆ Ignoring others or treating them with indifference
- ◆ Dishonesty
- ◆ Self-absorption
- ◆ Impulsive initial negative responses
- ◆ Disregarding the contributions and creativity of others

Relationship Success

In chapter 4, we discussed communication skills, which are intertwined with interrelational skills. Effective communication is essential to building productive workplace relationships, as is the mindset of treating everyone as a customer. Much has been written about the importance of external and internal customer service. It is important to see everyone you work with as a customer and deserving of the same service and respect as someone outside of the organization who would actually pay for your products or services. This is difficult to do, since we frequently take internal people for granted and often see them in an "us against them" antagonistic role. However, the same skills used to serve and maintain relationships with those outside your organization serve you well when applied internally.

You have a symbiotic relationship with external customers. You provide something they want (product or service) and they provide something you want (revenue, profit). This same relationship exists with your internal people. You need them and they need you. The importance of building and nurturing effective internal relationships with those above you in the organization is obvious, however, the necessity of establishing these same relationships with those who may be lateral or below you in the organization is frequently overlooked.

The first step in building successful internal or external customer relationships is discovering your customers' expectations and determining your ability to meet them.

An effective exercise to help you determine your internal and external customers' expectations is to facilitate a discussion asking them:

1. What do I do that helps you?

2. What do I do that hinders you?
3. What should I consider doing differently?

This exercise allows you to determine both their needs and their perception of your effectiveness. It also demonstrates your willingness to provide them with the exact quality of performance and interaction they require. This helps you to see your performance from their perspective, which can be a very enlightening vantage point.

Invest the Time to Build Relationships

Building and nurturing effective workplace relationships requires an active and creative dedication of your time. For example:

◆ Strategically use your lunch hour to seek out and spend time with others.
◆ Offer to help with activities or special projects.
◆ Volunteer or support extracurricular organizational services (United Way, company picnics, external fundraising, etc.).

Planning the time and actively developing the strategies that grow relationships and demonstrate your interrelational skills are as important to your quest for a successful promotion as the quality of your current technical performance.

Expand Your Sphere of Influence

Gain exposure to as many people as possible within your organization. In small organizations, this is relatively easy, but in larger ones, it is more challenging. Do not limit your workplace relationships to your immediate intimate work group. Penetrate as deeply into the organization as possible. If there is an organization-wide activity, participate. Offer to bring the potato salad or the ice for the picnic. Attend any organizationally sponsored nights at the ballpark, concerts, or the like.

Behave yourself! Unprofessional extracurricular behavior has a definite terminal effect on your career.

If there is a company-sponsored team playing softball, basketball, or any other sport, go to the games. If somebody's child is selling Girl Scout cookies or involved in a school fund-raiser, participate. When asked to be generous with your time or money, seek as many opportunities as you can to say yes. While participation is not mandatory, you may be conspicuous by your absence. Refusing to get involved is career "dumbness."

Treat Everyone with Dignity and Respect at All Times

While you don't always like all the people you work with (and frankly, they don't always like you), your personal feelings should never dictate your behavior or how you treat someone. Your coworkers should be unable to tell whether you truly like them or not. Your workplace behavior should be consistent for everyone.

Some of the ways in which dignity and respect can be defined are:

◆ Refrain from raising your voice or displaying any form of abusive, verbal or nonverbal behaviors.

◆ Never use inappropriate language.

◆ Avoid any comment or behavior bordering on harassment or discrimination.

◆ Never talk about people behind their backs.

◆ Listen to others even when you are in obvious disagreement.

◆ Avoid generally labeling people as being part of an undesirable group ("those second-shift people" or "the technical geeks!").

Displays of disrespect are not only damaging to the people bearing the brunt of the action, they are also visible to everyone around you, and lower your value in the eyes of others. The perception spreads that if you are willing to treat one person like that, then you are probably willing to treat everyone like that.

Be Truthful

Effective relationships are always anchored in truth, which means telling the truth as you know it to be at all times. It doesn't mean selectively withholding information or telling people what you think they want to hear. People need to know they can take what you say as gospel—not occasionally, but with a demonstrated consistency.

However, being truthful does not absolve you from the responsibility of using tact in your communications, or permit you to disregard someone else's feelings. Being truthful does not include the counterproductive behavior of someone who "tells it like it is" or "shoots from the hip" or enjoys telling people painful messages "for their own good." There are many hurtful and mean-spirited people who excuse their damaging behavior by qualifying it as statements of truth. Being truthful does not give you the right to hurt someone!

 Truth is always based in facts and details, not opinions, judgments or the perceptions of others.

If your conversations frequently start off with qualifying statements such as, "I'm going to tell you this for your own good" or "I don't know how to be anything but truthful, it's just the kind of person I am," you probably make a habit of offending people, leaving excessive amounts of damage in your wake. This is not effective promotable behavior!!!

Conveying the truth also means admitting when you don't know, and acknowledging confidential information that cannot be shared. Statements such as, "I'm not at liberty to discuss that and when I am I certainly will" or "This is not something I am comfortable discussing" may be temporarily frustrating to others, but in the long term, they reinforce your truthfulness, honesty, and integrity.

Follow-Through

As previously discussed, the importance of keeping your word and developing your reputation as someone who consistently does what you say you will do is always an integral part of any effective relationship. If you say you are going to do something—do it!

Show Personal Interest

No one wants to be seen as merely a meaningless interchangeable part. We all want to be treated as individuals and acknowledged for our uniqueness. This means taking a personal interest in those with whom you consistently interact. Extend compliments (appropriate to the workplace) and acknowledge their strengths whenever possible. Take an interest in their families or personal lives. Build bridges of commonality while celebrating and learning from any areas of difference. This calls heavily upon your listening skills, and your acceptance of those who see things from a perspective other than yours. Let people know that your relationship is not just defined by what they do, it is significantly impacted by who they are. Honor them as individuals.

Assess Relationships *vs.* Friendships

While the development and nurturing of successful internal workplace relationships are necessary to enhance your promotability, be wary of workplace friendships. This may seem controversial or harsh, so a real-world analytical look at workplace friendships might be helpful.

Always keep in mind that if your promotion objectives are reached, and your career growth proceeds, you will probably be in a position to manage or lead your current peers. Friendships established early in your career may create unforeseen future challenges (not necessarily caused by your inability to deal with the friendship, but theirs). When you manage friends, you may be objective and able to separate the roles, but they may not. Because you are considered a friend, they may expect special considerations, such as the relaxation of rules and policies, preference in work assignments, or unrealistic compensation considerations.

When you do not accommodate these or other inappropriate expectations, friendships frequently disintegrate, resentment escalates, and passive aggressive resistant behavior develops. Your friends may end up establishing themselves as your opposition. Frequently, they will accuse you of forgetting who your friends are, or treating them as inferior because of your career success.

The truth is, career growth will probably cost you friendships. Workplace friendships tend to be trees with shallow roots, usually based on proximity and convenience, that rarely have lasting influence when separation or realignment occurs. If you realistically assess your past workplace friends, you'll find few of them maintained their closeness when one or both of you transferred or moved on. How many of the old gang from the old days are really still your good buddies today?

 Today's workplace confidant may become tomorrow's adversary.

Commonly, you share frustrations, disappointments, or occasional negativity with workplace friends, but these can come back to haunt you. Avoid sharing any thoughts or feelings that you wouldn't want published in the organization's newsletter. The things you share in confidence may end up on the informal communication highway of the grapevine! The friend you are sharing these thoughts with today may be competing with you tomorrow for a new job. If you find yourself in future competitive or possibly antagonistic circumstances, events and recollections of the past may resurface and be turned against you.

There are times when we all need to vent and seek outlets for pent-up emotions, however, venting with workplace peers can be dangerous. Identify trustworthy people, external to your workplace, who will listen nonjudgmentally, perhaps offer advice, then throw their recollections to the wind when the discussion is over. If you do engage in workplace venting, any discussion must contain suggestions for solutions. If you are describing a problem and brainstorming solutions, then you are engaging in an appropriate discussion, however, if you are merely identifying problems and releasing emotions, then you are not. Today's venting session may be tomorrow's embarrassment, which may demand an apology or explanation.

 Do your venting outside of work.

Learn to Deal with Conflict

Dealing with conflict is a significant challenge for everyone in every workplace in America today. The fact is, we do not inherently resolve conflict well. We have adopted a style of avoidance. We tend to walk away from conflict, harbor seething resentments, and frequently plot ways of getting revenge rather than positively confronting the issue. We judge others harshly when they display these same behaviors, but of course, in our case, it's always justified. After all, they deserve it when we act this way because we are right and they are wrong! It's not uncommon for these unresolved conflicts to fester for extended periods of time, and while we refuse to discuss the issue with the party involved, we frequently discuss the conflict with many others who are neither involved nor in a position to resolve it. We try to increase our base of support by "back channelling," trying to build our case and draw others to our side. Discussions with the boss or perhaps the human resources department are frequently preceded with self-serving disclaimers of, "Don't tell her I told you this . . . but you better fix this." How's that for avoidance? We are not taught how to approach someone and interactively resolve conflict. Rarely do we learn these skills in our schools, in our family experiences, or in our workplace. The lack of conflict resolution training is a major gap in today's workplace skill development programs.

In my book, *The Bad Attitude Survival Guide: Essential Tools for Managers*, (Perseus, 1998) I devote two full chapters to the skills of conflict resolution. In regard to conflict resolution and your promotability, I would offer the following: while you may perceive the conflict to be entirely the fault of others, are you willing to allow their behavior or poor conflict resolution skills to negatively impact your promotability? Never give anyone that kind of negative control over your career.

 Learn to resolve conflict effectively and early. It takes no talent to dig in your heels and refuse to negotiate a positive outcome.

The costs of unresolved conflict on your career and the entire organization are staggering. In the face of unresolved conflict:

- ◆ Productivity declines.
- ◆ Passive aggressive resistant behaviors increase (subtle sabotage, cliquish alliances, character assassinations, etc.).
- ◆ Costly lawsuits are filed.
- ◆ Incidents of workplace violence escalate.

Ineffective Responses to Workplace Conflict
We tend to be in conflict when we perceive conditions of disrespect, unfairness, loss, or threat, and when someone tells us no or we don't get what we want! The typical negative responses to conflict situations in today's workplace are:

◆ **Avoidance.** Choosing to do nothing, holding the other person totally responsible, and allowing the conflict to escalate.

The issues continue, the emotions fester, and eventually a distorted overreactive response explodes.

◆ **Winning at all costs.** The perception that all conflicts must be won, and merely winning is not enough, the other party must be soundly defeated. They must know and acknowledge that they have been defeated, regardless of the significance of the issue. Total victory in all things at any cost!

◆ **Capitulation (surrender).** Giving in or giving up as quickly as possible—always being the one to make the accommodation, to take blame, and to be responsible for the correction. No matter what the circumstances, always give in, it's the best way to keep the peace. While this appears to be a successful way to resolve conflict early and avoid escalation, it is a seriously flawed strategy. Capitulators frequently hold resentment inside, allowing it to build and explode inappropriately at a later time.

These three responses are obviously all unproductive, and if you demonstrate them consistently, you will significantly reduce your chances of promotability.

Effective Responses to Workplace Conflict

Coping skills are unilateral behaviors. You elect to implement them totally on your own. You do not need the cooperation of the other party. These skills are effective for dealing with tolerable conflicts, such as:

◆ Misunderstandings	◆ Irritations
◆ Irrational behaviors	◆ Minor miscommunications
◆ Unintended slights	◆ Inconveniences
◆ Differences of opinion	◆ Disagreements on the interpretation of facts and data

The three primary coping skills are:

◆ **Tolerance.** Make a conscious decision to accept the conflict-causing behavior of others. It is an effective strategy for very low-level conflicts and requires a two-step process:

1. Acknowledge that the issue is relatively insignificant, does not have long-term detrimental potential, and ranks very low on a scale of 1 to 10.
2. Give it up. Do *not* hold the other person continuously responsible for the behaviors you have decided to tolerate. Simply put, stop keeping score! Tolerance is *not* quietly harboring resentment and waiting until the circumstance becomes so intolerable that you overreact, causing much greater conflict and disruption. You probably experience this frequently in your workplace. Someone finally explodes, and when they confront the other party, the first response is, "Why didn't you tell me about this earlier? Why was this allowed to become such a big issue when it could have been handled easily if I had known about it sooner?"

 Toleration is not delayed reaction—it is giving it up, getting over it, and moving on without harboring resentment!

◆ **Accommodation.** Accommodation is verbally acknowledged toleration. You make the decision to accommodate, however, you let the other person know you have. You may say to someone, "It works best for me if all the orders are processed by 3:00, but because 4:00 works best for you, I'm willing to adjust my routine to accommodate your schedule." (Be careful. Don't sit and angrily stew between 3:00 and 4:00 each day, waiting for the orders to be processed!)

The advantages of accommodation are that it makes others aware of what a nice person you are, and creates potential IOUs for future negotiations. The key to accommodation is letting people know you are doing it!

◆ **Delay.** Delay is another effective coping skill when time is an issue or when waiting a short time will help to reduce the conflict. If you are in crisis, peak season, or shorthanded, it may not be the time to address a minor conflict. If the passage of time will help the conflict resolve itself, it may be best to wait. The key to effective delay is to establish specific timelines.

Delays without timelines are nothing more than planned avoidance.

If you decide, "I'm going to wait until Stacey gets back from vacation and then talk with her," that would be an appropriate delay (providing you actually have the conversation upon her return). But failing to address the issue contributes to the buildup of unhealthy resentment and the conflict intensity will grow.

Another effective response to workplace conflict is interactive positive resolution, which contains elements of communication and problem-solving skills. This response entails active discussions with the conflicting party, the clear identification of issues, and the negotiation of positive joint solutions. The key to effective interactive positive resolution is to avoid personalization of the conflict by staying focused on what's happening, not who's doing it. Here are three techniques for avoiding personalization.

1. Use assertive communication pronouns (I/we) and avoid aggressive ones (you). Instead of "*You* are doing this . . . " the message becomes "Here is what *I* think is happening."
2. Eliminate any negative projections toward the other party. You frequently enter conflict perceiving your behaviors and motivations to be based in very positive, wholesome intentions. On the other hand, you perceive the conflicting party to be motivated by selfishness, greed, and other forms of felonious intent. Allow others to have their issues. Their issues are as legitimate to them as yours are to you. (Of course, they are wrong, but they have a right to their "flawed" perceptions.)

3. Refrain from historical references. Going "historical" during a conflict only escalates it and dredges up ghosts and unresolved issues of the past. Stay focused on today. What happened last year is really not relevant to what's happening now. Successful conflict resolution is a current event, not a history lesson.

> *A helpful guideline for conflict resolution is to stay focused on what must be accomplished, and be very flexible on how it will be accomplished.*

A Real-World Workplace Conflict Resolution Model

An effective eight-step process that successfully resolves conflict while simultaneously meeting the needs of everyone involved is:

1. Structure a positive opening/confronting phrase—"I think there is a problem and I'm sure that we can work it out."
2. State the problem assertively, unemotionally, and respectfully, using facts—"This is what I perceive is happening."
3. Ask for summarization/clarification—"I want to be sure I have communicated effectively. Help check me out. Summarize my perception."
4. Seek their perception—"Help me understand how you see this. What do you think is happening?"
5. Offer your summarization/clarification—"I want to be sure that I understand your position. This is what I heard you say, am I correct?"
6. Brainstorm options/agreements—"How can we work this out positively so that we can both meet our objectives?"
7. Commit to resolution.
   - ◆ Clarify responsibilities (who is going to do what).
   - ◆ Identify "how will we know?" (how will cooperation and success be measured?).

◆ Commit to a future meeting to discuss progress and results.

8. Remorse/reconsideration (making sure the resolution
   sticks).

   ◆ Allow a time for reflection (usually one hour, no more
     than twenty-four).
   ◆ Reconvene for a quick discussion to reaffirm agreement
     or further negotiation.
   ◆ Repeat step 7 to insure accurate comprehension.

Relationship Skills Assessment

	Yes	No
1. Do I limit my internal contacts and relationships to my intimate work group?	☐	☐
2. Do I specifically invest time in building workplace relationships?	☐	☐
3. Do I treat others in any way that may indicate a lack of dignity or respect?	☐	☐
4. Do I know the specific needs of my internal customers?	☐	☐
5. Do others perceive me as being untruthful or manipulative with the truth?	☐	☐
6. Do I take an appropriate personal interest in the people I work with?	☐	☐
7. Do I tend to vent or share criticisms with the people I work with?	☐	☐
8. Would I be able to manage or effectively lead my peers without the perception of violating friendships or turning my back on former confidants?	☐	☐
9. Do I tend to avoid dealing with workplace conflict?	☐	☐
10. Am I willing to listen and consider the opinions of others in conflict situations?	☐	☐
11. Do I tend to harbor resentment or ill feelings toward some people I work with or my boss?	☐	☐

12. Am I willing and able to discuss conflict issues in a positive, unemotional style that fosters resolution? □ □

Scoring:

Any *yes* responses to the odd-numbered questions or *no* responses to the even numbered questions demand your attention and a plan for improvement and development in order to increase your promotability. If you answered *no* to all of the odd questions and *yes* to all of the even questions—take a second look. A dose of reality may help overcome a probable case of denial!!

Building a Successful Relationship with Your Boss

Cultivating a strong professional relationship with your boss is an integral part of any promotion strategy. Your boss can be your greatest PR advocate or can hold you back, perhaps permanently. Whether trumpeting your strengths, skills, abilities, and willingness to everyone who will listen, or emphasizing your weaknesses and failures, your boss is going to play a pivotal role in your promotability. Is your boss an asset to be nurtured or an antagonist to be neutralized?

Boss/Relationship Assessment

	Yes	No
1. Does your boss assess and acknowledge your strengths reasonably, realistically, and appropriately?	□	□
2. Does your boss emphasize and criticize your weaknesses?	□	□
3. Does your boss rate and assess your fairly on your performance appraisals?	□	□
4. Is your boss proactive in offering training or strategies for improvement?	□	□
5. Is your boss supportive of your efforts in pursuing professional development?	□	□

	Yes	No

6. Does your boss appear to be threatened by your performance and achievements? ☐ ☐

7. Does your boss cooperate in creating opportunities for cross-functional interaction with other departments, teams, or areas? ☐ ☐

8. Does your boss routinely delegate critical, important, urgent tasks? ☐ ☐

9. Does your boss appear to single you out inappropriately for boring, repetitive, low-priority tasks? ☐ ☐

10. Does your boss appear to favor others in your department, team, or work group over you? ☐ ☐

11. Is there evidence that your boss shares positive information about you throughout the organization? ☐ ☐

12. Is there evidence that your boss shares negative information about you through-out the organization? ☐ ☐

Yes responses to questions 2, 6, 9, 10, and 12, and any *no* responses to other questions indicate negative signs and could be areas of concern in your relationship with your boss.

It is extremely important to realistically assess your relationship with your boss. Do not lull yourself into complacency with flowery promises that are not reinforced by actual supportive behaviors. Conversely, do not reactively judge your boss harshly if you are not totally supported in every endeavor or always given what you want. Take a long, hard, objective look at your working relationship and determine how to develop it to the best of your promotability.

Be Aware of the Boss's Formal and Informal Agendas

What does your boss want to accomplish? What formal objectives have been established for him? What are his primary responsibilities? How can you help him achieve his objectives? This is not just making your boss look good; it means becoming an asset to him in his overall effectiveness. Can you discover his informal agenda? What does he want for himself in his short-term and long-term futures? What is his preferred career path? Does he wish to stay where he is indefinitely (obviously, if you're trying to obtain his job, it could be problematic!), continue to climb upward on his current course, or does he intend to pursue opportunities in other areas? The more you know about what your boss wants to accomplish, the more you can position yourself to be of assistance.

Always Be Sensitive to Your Boss's Timelines

Never be the reason your boss is criticized or judged harshly for missing a deadline. Complete all of your responsibilities promptly, especially those influencing her performance, and always make yourself available to assist her in any additional way if timelines become tight. Position yourself as an ally.

 Being the reason your boss looks bad is not a good thing.

Always Keep Your Boss Informed

Embrace a personal policy of no surprises. Keep your boss informed of important developments, beginnings, endings, problems, and any relevant rumors that may be circulating on the grapevine (especially those pertaining to him or his responsibilities). Exercise caution not to expose or betray your sources of information when making your boss aware of anything relevant. It's also extremely important to inform your boss early of any problems. As we discussed earlier, the timing of your information can be the difference between your boss being an ally or an antagonist. Timing is everything.

Practice Upward Recognition

While we frequently communicate all of the things that are going wrong, we rarely tell the boss when things are going right. Just as you thrive on appropriate positive recognition, so does she. Be sure that your boss receives the appropriate "thank you," "nice going," and any positive press she deserves. Recognition is a two-way street.

Learn to Accept Criticism and Critical Comment

Easier said than done. We all have an aversion to hearing information that may not be complimentary or is critical of our performance. As unlikely as it may seem, you are not perfect, and from time to time, it will be appropriate for someone to offer critical comment on your work or behavior. Your boss may counsel you to change embedded or developing habits, and this feedback actually helps you to grow if you accept it appropriately. It also gives you the opportunity to discover the perceptions of others and identify the necessary corrective action to increase your promotability.

 Criticism, critical comments, or negative feedback are gifts—they will help you improve.

Don't take criticism personally. Interpret your boss's comments as identified problems, not personal attacks. It's not about you, it's some *thing* you may or may not be doing. It's not about you, it's a change he deems necessary. It's not about you, it's behavior interpreted to be detrimental and he is giving you a gift of developmental feedback.

An effective five-step process for effectively receiving criticism or critical comment:

1. Listen, depersonalize—repeat to yourself, "This is not about me, it's a problem, not personal."

2. Assertively restate the comments for clarification—
"What I heard was that this (behavior or work) is not acceptable."
3. Seek guidance—"How could I do that differently? What change would be appropriate?"
4. Process the input—Determine the validity of the comments and assess your willingness to eliminate the contention and implement the change.
5. Review/reinforce—Seek every opportunity to demonstrate your willingness to embrace the change, and after an appropriate period of time, seek a follow-up conversation to determine your boss's perception of your progress. "I'm working hard to bring about that change. I'd like to know if you think I'm successful, or have any suggestions for what else I can do."

Learning to accept and grow from critical comments is a challenge that will demonstrate your maturity and your readiness for promotion.

Becoming defensive or initiating an intimidating counterattack of someone offering critical comment or criticism is easy. While we expect everyone else to be able to accept critical comment, we frequently do not hold ourselves to the same standard.

Dealing with a Difficult Boss

Most bosses aren't as bad as some people choose to perceive, but there are some bad ones out there. Even if your boss is one of the bad ones, she is a study of organizational success. She is doing something right. You don't get to be the boss by being dumb! Even a bad boss offers significant learning opportunities. Observe your boss's behaviors and determine what you can emulate to enhance your promotability. Try to put personal feelings aside and objectively assess the situation. It is quite possible your boss is a product of the prevailing organizational culture. If you want to succeed in that culture, your boss may offer a blueprint.

Abusive, Discriminatory, or Harassing Behaviors

If your boss is practicing abusive, discriminatory, or harassing behaviors, you must distance yourself from even the appearance of any involvement or culpability. In no way be seen as supporting or cooperating in any unacceptable, unethical, or perhaps illegal behaviors. If you are the recipient of these actions from your boss, it is imperative that you:

◆ Accurately document all incidents.
◆ Positively confront your boss with your thoughts and evidence in an attempt to resolve it personally and quietly.
◆ Pursue correction through the appropriate formal organizational channels if personal resolution is unacceptable.

Policies and procedures for addressing these problems are specifically identified within the organization, and if not, they certainly should be. The human resource department or upper management should be made aware of the problem and be involved with the correction in an expedient and professional manner. Keep detailed records of all contacts, conversations, and instructions, even though confronting these circumstances is unpleasant and could perhaps damage your career if you are labeled as a troublemaker. Keep things in their proper perspective. No job or promotion is worth enduring unethical or illegal treatment or activities. If the organization is unresponsive to your predicament, you really do not want to continue your employment there. Why would you want to pursue a promotion in that environment?

When You Truly Have a Bad Boss

There are three options or courses of action if you have a "bad" boss.

1. Negotiate for change

This negotiation can take two forms. Have an interactive dialogue with your boss to present your perceptions, incorporating the communication, problem-solving, and conflict resolution steps previously outlined in this book. Take care to insure depersonalization of all issues and maintain a factual and detailed discussion supported by your documentation. Offer solutions, not just problems or criticisms, and negotiate resolutions. If this dialogue degenerates into an emotional outburst or a blaming session, you lose.

The negotiation for change may also involve others higher in the management chain or perhaps the human resource department. This step should only be taken *after* you have tried a serious intervention strategy directly with your boss. Be aware, involving others in problems with your boss can be a risk-plagued strategy, and should not be undertaken without considerable thought.

 If you win, it can help your career; if you lose, it will sink promotability!

Taking problems over your boss's head will invoke a predictable defensive response. He will proclaim you to be a troublemaker, and perhaps paint a picture of you that no other manager will want to embrace. He is going to defend himself and he may have the power and influence to insure victory in this type of battle. Even if you win this incident, you may ultimately lose the war. Many bad bosses have long memories.

Is it ever the right thing to involve others? Of course, however, do not pursue this strategy without significant thought and consideration of risk.

2. Accept it

This strategy accepts the reality of the situation and acknowledges that although uncomfortable or nonidyllic, it is tolerable and it is in your best interest to deal with it. There is no such thing as a perfect job or a perfect boss, and it could be best to concede that your options or influence may be limited. Do *not* adopt this coping strategy without first seeking to negotiate change directly with your boss. If you just accept it without attempting to change the situation first, you are choosing to avoid the problem, and your tension and resentment will severely escalate. This may result in a future blowup or negative display of emotion, which could cost you your job or severely diminish your promotability.

Do not vent to coworkers or friends about how bad your boss is. Any breach of coworker confidentiality could be deadly, and venting to friends doesn't help you. To support you they will listen and agree. While this reinforces your feelings and perceptions, it may only serve to escalate a self-righteous indignation on your part, which only makes things worse.

 Be wary of the advice of others. It is very easy for someone else to quit your job or tell you what they would say to your boss!!

If you do decide to accept your current circumstance with your bad boss and attempt to ride it out, it may be in your best interest to seek some outside help or counseling (perhaps through the Employee Assistance program, your faith affiliation, or other resources available within your community). Find some professional guidance for minimizing the stress or negative effect the bad boss has on you.

Guidance from professionals can help you to implement effective strategies for minimizing the damage. If you do not take specific steps to balance the bad boss' influence positively, he will probably take you down. Don't let the bad boss win!

3. Relocate

Seek a transfer, reassignment, or change jobs. Obviously, if your goal is to achieve promotion in your current position, relocation would be a painful decision to make. Look at this option with extreme caution. Relocation may actually be running from the problem and can become a patterned behavior of choice for some. While it may be necessary, it rarely results in personal growth. If you choose relocation, be sure that you execute the change in a well-planned, nonemotional way and do not just accept the first opportunity that comes along. Do not let a bad boss manipulate you into an impulsive career-damaging move.

The Four Ps

Realizing that effective workplace relationships are critical to any promotion strategy, here are some additional moves that will help impact how others view you and your promotability.

Learn Not to Demonstrate or Vocalize Your Initial Negative Response

In the face of negative information or a bad event, learn not to give voice or nonverbal expression to your potentially negative response. Others will see your negative response and may, in turn, react poorly to you. These initial responses are impulsive, emotional, subjective, and void of thought. An effective strategy is to learn to give them the test of time before you react (the old count to ten isn't bad). If at all possible, invoke the ninety-minute rule, which is to give yourself time to process the event and your response before you react. Say to yourself, "I'm going to see how I feel about this in ninety minutes and then I will react appropriately to the situation."

Obviously, this is not always possible, especially in the face of a crisis. However, the more you exercise control over any negative, knee-jerk response to people or issues, the more you present yourself as mature, controlled, and above such reactionary impulsive behavior. (You will also have fewer apologies to make!)

People will take your comments or input more seriously because they are based on ninety minutes of thought, not one-tenth of a second of emotion.

Avoid the Negative Feeding Frenzies

The national pastime in America is no longer baseball—it has become whining and complaining (just listen to talk radio!). When others engage in these behaviors, take care not to be drawn in or perceived as part of the negativity. Either distance yourself quickly or attempt to refocus them on positive alternatives and options. Do not just listen without responding, they will perceive your silence to be agreement and it may be assumed that you are a part of the negative flock. Silence is not good enough, you may be guilty by association. React positively, move away, and refuse to be sucked in. "I don't like talking about all this negative stuff. I'm going to finish my report."

Make yourself a more attractive candidate for promotion by developing your positive attributes and by not participating in negative carping.

Avoid Cronyism and Cliques

Any shows of favoritism for one group of people over another, us against them, or in-crowd/out-crowd, put you in a vulnerable position. While it may be to your advantage to be a part of the in-group, power and influence can shift, and rather quickly. For example, when there are changes of leadership in many organizations, there is a subsequent flurry of re-jockeying of position, as people who were once part of the in-crowd attempt to maintain their position and those who were previously out attempt to acquire more influence. Position yourself as inclusively as possible, avoiding any potentially polarizing alignments. Collaborate and cooperate with all and shun none.

Take Advantage of Your Networking Contacts

Call in favors on behalf of others. If someone needs information or special help from an area where you have developed strong networking alignments, be willing to use your relationships on their behalf. What you do for others is an investment that will pay great future dividends. Showcase the depth of your network, and your eagerness to use your contacts. Nurture the perception of yourself as someone who has access and can get things done.

Celebrate and Learn from the Success of Others

Petty jealousies won't get you promoted. The success of someone else is a learning opportunity for you. Celebrate the success of others and attempt to learn as much as you can from their achievements. Never be seen as resenting or feeling threatened by the success of others.

There are many examples of successful career strategies in your organization. What can you learn from them? How can you model these successes?

Always Maintain Confidentiality

If you are personally entrusted with confidential information or your position exposes you to sensitive documents, never violate that trust. You must be seen as a person capable and willing to manage confidential and sensitive information and your peers must perceive you as someone who will not violate their trust. Never put yourself in a position to be the unnamed source of leaks or the root of confidentiality violations. Relationships disintegrate in the face of violated confidences. If you prove to be unable to control your disclosures, you will probably not be seriously considered for positions of increased responsibility.

Maintain Zero Tolerance for the Undignified and Disrespectful Treatment of Others

This applies not only to your own behavior, but the behavior of others as well. If an individual or group becomes the brunt of jokes, be sure that your discomfort is known. Visibly display your displeasure and unwillingness to accept the ridicule or denigration of others. An effective response might be, "I don't think those comments/jokes are appropriate in the workplace. Let's see if we can talk about something else." Always insist that dignity and respect be maintained, whether others are present or not. If emotions erupt and disrespectful behavior comes into play, handle it by saying, "Let's take a few minutes for all of us to calm down, and then we will resume our discussion." Be seen as someone who consistently travels the high road.

Help Others Find Success in Failure

When others experience a failed or disrupted project, help them salvage any possible positive outcome that may have occurred. Emphasize learning opportunities, group work for future success, or contacts that may have been made. No matter how bad the actual outcome, something good can be found if you dig deep enough. Help others to focus on the good. If nothing else, help them to see the bad event as temporary, something to be dealt with, put behind them, and left in their rearview mirror.

 Reinforcing failure or engaging in "catastrophizing" serves no purpose.

Give Others Permission to Disagree with You

Not everyone thinks like you do, and they have a right to think how they choose. Encourage disagreement and debate. Divergent opinion is a healthy dynamic for any relationship, and being seen as a stifler of dissent decreases your promotability. Acknowledging disagreement does not mean you are changing your position, it merely affirms the difference of opinion. Be willing to give others a forum for their ideas, and demonstrate your flexibility by allowing yourself to be "converted" if appropriate. Be seen by others as a person who welcomes divergent thought.

Stay Focused on *What* Must Be Done and Allow Others to Have Significant Influence on *How* It Is to Be Accomplished

Give others as much input or control as possible over how they are going to do something. If the final outcome is successful, meets the standards of quality, time, and dollars, who cares *how* it's actually done! Your primary concern is with the final outcome. Allowing others to determine how it is to be accomplished increases their commitment and encourages them to collaborate with you on future opportunities.

 People don't argue with themselves or their own ideas!

Stimulate the Creativity of Others

Continuously repeat the mantra, "What if we tried this a different way? Is there another way of accomplishing this task that would increase efficiency? Lower cost? Create less hassle?" Be seen as someone who is always seeking a better way to improve the organization and the quality of work life for everyone, and is willing to involve others in the process. Seek ways to help others expand their horizons and think outside the box.

Real-World Promotion Mentoring

Barbara Mauntler is the Manager of Organization Effectiveness and Training for the Midwestern Business Unit of Sun Oil Co. in Toledo, Ohio. We asked Barbara to describe the types of training programs her department is being asked to provide for preparing the organization's employees for future success. She responded:

> *Our organization has been heavily technically focused and concentrated on developing people's technical competence over the years. Our executives are realizing that we need to develop people's leadership and business competence at levels much lower into the organization. We are being asked to focus on these competencies even though we are a highly technical organization. We are developing leadership skills, including being able to facilitate and build teams, interpersonal communication, negotiating, facilitating, delegating, problem solving, and effective conflict resolution, along with business competencies like financial understanding for nonfinancial people, industry economics, and so on. We are focusing on turning our technical people into businesspeople and leaders.*

When asked whom she would recommend as a mentor to someone seeking promotion, Barbara offered these thoughts.

> *The first thing I would say is find someone you trust who is high enough in the organization to give you honest and frank feedback regarding the kinds of things that you're doing right, as well as what other people may see as impeding your career. These could range from technical competencies to interpersonal issues or any kind of skill or ability gap. My experience in human resources has been that people's shortcomings are identified very easily in conversations with everyone but them, and when their career has stalled and they have no idea why. Once this information is gained, then find resources to help overcome those deficiencies. People can find someone who is good at things where they are weak to help mentor them or they can find other resources through self-study materials, books, tapes, videos, classes, or by simply observing other people who demonstrate those strengths. I also think seeking rotational temporary assignments is a really good career-developing move. A lot of times they are just lateral moves, but they fill in your gaps, and these new opportunities may give you visibility in*

the organization and allow for you to make a unique contribution that no one else has made.

Barbara also places great emphasis on presentation skills.

You can be very technically sharp, bright, and make contributions to the bottom line, but if you can't communicate what you're doing and feel comfortable, particularly around higher management, then you're going to have promotion difficulties. I think presentation skills, including selling skills, are really critical in terms of getting upper management to take notice of you and understand the work that you're bringing to the organization.

Barbara also expressed her thoughts on the importance of sharing recognition and developing others. She stressed the importance of not taking credit for other's work and making sure that everyone receives acknowledgment. She said:

If it's a we kind of an effort, you have to be very careful to give credit where credit is due. The managers that I've seen actually promoted have been interested in promoting other people and making sure that they are grooming their replacements. It's sort of an ironic twist that if you develop others, you're going to create opportunities for yourself to move on. Often people are not promoted because there is no one to fill their spot and they get stuck. So actually the people I've seen get promoted are people who are really big on developing others.

Barbara went on to say:

I think creating career opportunities for themselves is a particular challenge for women. Women focus on doing the job they're in extremely well, while men tend to focus on the next step. I think women really need to pay attention to growing their replacements and keeping their eye on the next job as well as doing their current job well. Often they tend to focus too much on doing their current job perfectly and don't give enough thought to where it's going to take them.

In closing, Barbara offered these thoughts:

Self-motivation is a key component in career advancement. I really think that a positive and enthusiastic attitude is a great determiner of how people view you and whether you're considered an asset to a project, team, or to the company. Then that enthusiasm has to be backed up with substantive contributions. When an individual has both those things going for them, they are viewed as a high-potential employee. I try to surround myself with other people who are enthusiastic and positive and who are problem solvers, not just complainers and problem makers. I think if you surround yourself with other positive people, it's catching. I try to stay away from people who are down-in-the-mouth, depressed, and discouraged.

Barbara obviously believes that exceptional interrelational skills, coupled with top personal performance and the ability to communicate effectively, are the foundations to promotability. She also mentioned the importance of self-motivation. In chapter 8 we address the critical component of maintaining a positive focus and keeping yourself motivated. People who are highly promotable do not rely on others to motivate them. They develop intense internal motivation that carries them to the top.

SELF-MOTIVATION

Jason was with a sales organization for approximately two years. It was his first job since college graduation, and while at times he found himself highly motivated and anxious to perform his job well, he also experienced periods of high frustration, low motivation, and frequent discouragement. As a successful college athlete, he was accustomed to being constantly motivated by his coaches. Now Jason found himself resentful when his current boss wasn't playing that same role. In a conversation driven by frustration with his manager, Jason said, "You're not doing your job. You're my manager, you're supposed to motivate me, and I am not motivated to do this job well. Sometimes I don't even feel like coming to work and you need to do something about that." Jason's boss thought for a moment and pointed to a picture of his mother prominently displayed in the adjacent bookcase. He said, "Jason, do you see the woman in that picture? That's my mother, and you need to realize that she did not go through the pangs of childbirth and give life to me so that someone would be on this earth to motivate you. We are all responsible for our own motivation. I am happy to help you achieve whatever motivates you, but do not expect me to provide your motivation. I have all I can do to keep myself motivated. You either wake up each day with that fire in your belly to do the job well or you don't. Over the long haul no one else can give you that fire!"

Many people like Jason perceive their motivation to be the responsibility of others. Parents, teachers, and coaches may help to provide this motivation early in life, but in today's workplace the day-to-day motivation necessary to achieve promotion must come from within.

While there are people who are good external motivators, stimulating to listen to, instilling the desires for changed behavior and exceptional performance, their motivation is usually very short-term. The "win one for the Gipper" kind of appeal is effective when goals are short-term, but for long-term goals such as increasing your overall performance and getting promoted, that type of motivation is inconsequential. Short-term emotional appeal does not achieve long-term goal satisfaction.

Your motivation is your own responsibility. If you are relying on others to keep you focused and in a state of high readiness to perform, you are going to be sorely disappointed in the long run. Do not give others so much power or influence over you by allowing them to be responsible for your motivation and desire. Doing so makes you extremely vulnerable to the negative intentions or manipulations of others.

 The person responsible for motivating you looks back at you every time you look in the mirror.

Here are some strategies to consider for developing the skills of self-motivation.

Define Long-Term Goals

Perhaps the most solid foundation for becoming highly motivated is to clearly define your long-term goals and keep your eye on the ultimate prize. The realization that your career growth and development are long-term endurance challenges, not short-term sprints, helps you sustain motivation and minimize the day-to-day bumps in the road. If your goals are short-term, your motivation is inconsistent and in constant need of replenishment. You set a goal, you accomplish it quickly, and then you must ask yourself, "Now what should I do?" Recreating goals and motivation becomes a constantly draining challenge. When goals are viewed for the long term, motivation is consistent and easier to sustain. Determined and steady wins the race.

In the pace and pressure of today's workplace, you frequently ask yourself the magic questions: "Why am I doing this? Why am I working so hard? Why am I doing so much more than others?" If you don't have long-term goals you can't answer these questions satisfactorily, and the result is an automatic and severe drop in your motivation. When your goals provide committed answers to these questions, the day-to-day frustrations and setbacks are minimized and they become mere speed bumps on the road of life.

Compete with Yourself

Yes, you have internal competitors within the organization, specifically those who seek the same opportunities and promotions that you do. It's easy to become discouraged if you perceive others as having skills and abilities superior to your own or in stronger political positions. These perceptions can quickly generate a decrease in your self-motivation. In reality, you cannot control the skills, abilities, and positioning of the people around you—you can only control your own! You really are not competing with them, you are competing with yourself. Your challenge is to increase the quality of your performance each day. Focusing on things you control dramatically increases your motivation. Agonizing about things over which you have no control erodes your self-motivation. The choice is yours.

Your number one competitor looks back at you every time you look in the mirror.

Celebrate Your Success

As you strive to improve your performance and position yourself for promotion, never lose sight of the importance of celebrating how successful you already are. Acknowledge your current high level of performance and acknowledge your past achievements. Can you get better? Of course, but the truth is, "you ain't all that bad now." Even though your journey may be long, your performance is better today than it was yesterday, last week, last month, last year.

 Internal criticism is the fast track to de-motivation.

Constantly saying to yourself, "I've got to get better, I've got to get better, I've got to get better" without taking the time to celebrate how competent you already are, continually reinforces the negative message, "I'm not good enough, I'm not good enough, I'm not good enough."

If a pole-vaulter routinely clears eight feet and wants to improve to consistently exceed ten feet, he does not raise the bar two feet all at once. No one is capable of improving performance to that degree in one fell swoop. The bar is moved from eight feet to eight feet two inches. Clearing it the first time is a one-time event, but clearing it two additional times in succession makes it the new standard level of performance. Then he celebrates the achievement and moves the bar up two more inches! He *incrementally* challenges himself to improve. Achieving a two-foot performance increase actually offers twelve opportunities to celebrate success when it is done two inches at a time! It is easier to be motivated in a climate of ongoing success and celebration than one of constant criticism or disappointment.

Maintaining high levels of self-motivation can be difficult in a culture that frequently denigrates those who don't finish first. Consider the prevailing attitude that "second place is nothing but first loser." Do you see yourself as a loser if you finish in second place? Or do you celebrate the success of your second place finish and then rededicate yourself to improving and winning the next time? People who finish second aren't losers . . . they are successful people faced with challenges to improve. People who are unmotivated or too intimidated to try again fall into the loser category! The more you focus on self-criticism, the more elusive your motivation will be. Concentrate on what you are and what you can become, not what you aren't.

The more you celebrate your successes, the more self-motivated you will become.

Keep Frustrations and Bad Experiences in a Positive Perspective

Disappointments, frustrations, and failures are everyday components of today's workplace. Things don't always go your way and you don't always get everything you want. Crises, problems, and pressing deadlines are frustrating, however, it is important to keep negative experiences from dominating your outlook. While these realities are predictable and inevitable, allowing yourself to be miserable or controlled by them is a conscious choice and one that can be refused. W. Mitchell, one of the most popular and effective motivational speakers in America today, trumpets as his signature message, "It's not what happens to you in life. It's how you choose to deal with it."[4] He is an individual who has experienced tragic circumstances, suffering debilitating and disfiguring injuries that would have destroyed many, yet he has triumphed over major adversities and experienced great success by maintaining a positive perspective concerning all of his challenges.

In his book, *Learned Optimism*, Dr. Martin Seligman observes that positive optimistic people tend to interpret bad events as being temporary and specific, refusing to see them as permanent or pervasive.[5] It is critical to your self-motivation to realize that your disappointments, frustrations, and failures are not all encompassing, but are limited very specifically to certain events and areas. If a project doesn't go well it doesn't mean that everything you touch fails. Acknowledge the bad and concentrate on the abundance of good. See problems as challenges to be successfully dealt with, and put behind you. Constantly remind yourself that "this too shall pass." Perceiving problems to be insurmountable or ongoing destroys motivation.

As previously discussed, the importance of identifying all available options for dealing with challenges, frustrations, and disappointments is extremely important in helping you maintain self-motivation. Victims are people who see themselves as having no options, influence, or control. Victimization creates *de*-motivation.

Commit to Three Daily Motivation Boosters

What quick (less than ten minutes) activity can you do to help motivate yourself? For some it may be:

- Reading a motivating book
- Reviewing skill-development information
- Listening to a motivational tape
- Spiritual reading, listening, or prayer

Identify your quick motivator and repeat it at least three times each day:

- In the morning before leaving for work
- Mid-morning (10:00–10:30 A.M.)
- Mid-afternoon (2:30–3:00 P.M.)

Short-burst motivators refocus your mindset and provide an uplifting boost. (It beats the caffeine rush of coffee!)

Courtney is a mid-level manager in a banking organization. Her persona is very conservative in dress and action. She plays classical music continuously in her office to help her concentrate and maintain an image of style, taste, and the like. Interestingly, at least twice each day she closes her office door, dons a headset and blasts five minutes of her favorite rock and roll oldies into her brain. She says, "It really helps get the blood pumping and motivates me to meet the challenges of the day head on!" What can you do to consistently replenish your motivation? It's nobody's responsibility but yours!

Nurture Yourself Physically

The link between your physical self and your motivation cannot be denied. If you fail to care for yourself physically, your motivation and positive attitude are the first things to go, followed quickly by performance. It is extremely difficult to be motivated when you feel tired or physically incapable of meeting your challenges.

The four primary considerations for maintaining your physical edge are: diet, rest, exercise, and avoiding abusive habits.

Abusive Habits

Any abuse relating to substance or behavior habits will do severe long-term damage to your health and career. While "all things in moderation" might be appropriate in some circumstances, anything bordering on illegal will not only hurt you physically, but any subsequent legal complications could sabotage your career growth permanently. Use your judgment; don't con yourself with denial, and if you need help, go get it.

 Being suspected of substance abuse or illegal activity can kill your career. Avoid even the appearance of impropriety.

Manage Stress Effectively

Stress management is critical to your performance, success, and promotability. If the reality or the perception exists that you are overstressed or unable to deal with the pressures of your current position, it's a real stretch to think that others would consider you for more demanding assignments. Some techniques that will help you address the issues of workplace stress follow.

Analyze Your Stress

Analyze the root causes of your stress. The causes are different for every individual. Do you know what yours are? Is your stress rooted in:

- Changing work demands?
- Individual people?
- Complications in your personal life?
- Financial pressures?
- Overwhelmingly urgent deadlines?

When you diagnose the main contributors to your stress, you can begin to develop effective prevention and corrective strategies. Diagnosis is the key.

Anticipate Stress

What can you do differently to plan your response to potentially stressful situations? If you know what increases your stress, how can you prepare yourself to limit your exposure to react differently when faced with that stressful reality? By planning ahead, you can choose proactive behavioral responses rather than react negatively and impulsively to the situation.

Pick Your Battles

Learn to determine the difference between a raging four-alarm fire and a burnt marshmallow! Not every circumstance is worth challenging, and not every battle is worth fighting. Choose wisely. If a circumstance is truly important to you, then address it in a planned, mature way. Prioritize by importance and impact. Learn to assess and be willing to let go of incidents or situations that just don't matter. "Don't sweat the minutiae."

Take the Time to Play

Maintain positive diversions in your life. Keep family, personal, and workplace issues in balance. When one leg of a table is a different length, the table obviously becomes unbalanced. Our lives are the same. While at any given moment certain segments of our lives take priority and may demand intense attention, the lasting emphasis of one over the others can do long-term damage. Maintain a healthy balance and have some fun!

All work and no play makes you an idiot—and not much fun to be around!

Reject Personal Perfection

Do not put pressure on yourself to be perfect. Perfectionism is a state that cannot be maintained and ultimately consumes those who try. Mistakes are not proof of personal weakness or incompetence. Mistakes are indicators that growth and development are necessary, and provide an opportunity for learning. Just as you admire others who are willing to take risks and learn from their mistakes, offer that same admiration and opportunity to yourself.

The self-perceived need for personal perfection frequently inhibits the willingness to take initiative and risk, which does not increase promotability.

Choose Positive Relationships

There are people around you who are extremely positive, creative, and lift your spirits. They contribute to your motivation. Develop relationships with them, seek their counsel, and spend as much discretionary time as possible in their presence. These are the people who tend to be consistently successful, enthusiastic, positively self-motivated, and their demeanor is contagious. Increase your exposure to the good guys.

Manage the Difficult People Successfully

Some people bring you up, and some people bring you down. Distance yourself as much as possible from the negative people in your environment. Those who continuously whine, complain, and criticize others ultimately have a very negative effect on you. They will eventually take you down. It's difficult to see the change, because it is the equivalent of the ocean eroding the beach. You don't see anything different on a day-to-day basis, but when you observe it year-to-year, you witness a significant amount of erosion. Your self-motivation and positive attitude are extremely valuable prime beachfront property, and the negative people around you are trying to steal your beach. Don't let them do it. Difficult people, whether their behavior is intentional or not, can be significant de-motivators. Developing your skills to neutralize their potentially damaging impact on you makes life a whole lot easier.

 Do not allow difficult people to control or negatively influence your perspective, performance, or promotability.

Defensive People

There is an awful lot of defensive behavior in today's workplace. Typical examples of defensive behavior include denying responsibility, claiming ignorance or the lack of information, blaming others, or claims of being unfairly targeted or singled out. Defensive people have also made an art form out of pleading innocent to crimes of which they haven't even been accused. If you ask them why particular tasks weren't done, they respond by telling you how many hours they work, how stressed they are, and how no one works as hard as they do. They don't want to talk about the uncompleted tasks, so they try to talk about everything else under the sun. In reality, defensive behavior is nothing more than changing the agenda of the discussion. They don't like the current topic so they divert attention elsewhere by using provocative, redirecting statements and behaviors.

While defensive people are very frustrating, they are relatively easy to neutralize.

- ◆ Never argue with them or tell them they are wrong (that is what they want you to do). Their behavior is intended to provoke you, and when you react, they have successfully changed the agenda!
- ◆ Never ignore their statements. If you do, they think you didn't hear them and they keep repeating them (usually more loudly) until they force you to respond.
- ◆ Never agree with defensive people. If you do, they win and the discussion is over with no positive outcome for you.

The most effective strategy is to acknowledge and refocus. Acknowledge their issue and refocus them on yours. "Eric, if you want to have a discussion about how hard you work, I'll be happy to talk about that as soon as we talk about the task that wasn't completed yesterday." Acknowledge their issues in a nonjudgmental, nonsarcastic, or noncondescending tone of voice and refocus them on your topic of discussion. When completed, offer to discuss their issues. Rarely do they want to actually discuss the points they have raised. Their issues are usually bogus and intended only to distract you. When unable to distract you, the issues are of no further value.

Typically, after three or four separate, successful episodes of acknowledging and refocusing, the defensive behavior stops. Once people realize it doesn't work, they stop being defensive.

Manipulative People

There are four primary behaviors that manipulative people use to influence and maneuver you into agreements or accommodations.

Appeals to Guilt

For many manipulators the motto is, "When all else fails, use guilt." Appeals to guilt are usually history lessons intended to make you give in or accommodate the issue of the moment because you *owe* them something for all they have done for you in the past. They reference previous actions and imply that you are uncaring, unfair, and ungrateful for not giving in to them now. Appeals to guilt are irrational establishments of after-the-fact quid pro quos when you are unaware there even was a quid pro quo! "Because I did this for you back when, you should do this for me now."

The most effective way to deal with appeals to guilt is to insist on remaining in the present, focusing only on the current situation. This is very similar to the acknowledge and refocus technique implemented with defensive people. "If you would like to talk about all of the things that you have done for me in the past, I would be very happy to talk about those as soon as we address this current situation."

 Always keep the conversation current when dealing with appeals to guilt.

Inappropriate Emotional Demonstrations

These are emotional demonstrations that are inappropriate, predictable, consistent, and implemented as a controlling behavior. This is not to imply that everyone who becomes emotional is attempting to be manipulative. Spontaneous emotional displays are very real and you want to help others regain their composure, refocus their thoughts, and deal rationally with the situation. Inappropriate emotional demonstrations are the temper tantrums, tears, or displays of grief that are used habitually as tactics for exiting uncomfortable situations or bringing an end to unpleasant conversations. The practitioners have learned that these techniques can be extremely effective and relatively easy to use. Temper tantrums are usually intended to intimidate you so that you will back off, and tears or grief are intended to make you refrain from upsetting the alleged victim even further. The effective response to these inappropriate emotional displays is to allow them to run their course, offer a very short period of recovery time, and continue on. It is important to allow them to cause only a short delay, not permanently end the unwanted experience.

In response to a temper tantrum, you might say: "Obviously, you are upset. Take a minute to compose yourself, and we will renew this discussion again in about ten minutes." Or, "If it helps you to get your emotions out, then by all means do so, and then we will address the issue."

In response to tears or displays of grief, you might say: "This is obviously upsetting. Please take some time to compose yourself and I'll be back in five minutes or so." If it is appropriate to leave the person alone for a short period, it is best for you to leave, not her. If she leaves and her emotional display becomes visible to others, it will generate support and sympathy and probably enhance her intensity. Keep her isolated. You leave, she composes herself, and then you continue.

The most important point in dealing with inappropriate emotional displays is not to allow them to end conversations. Temporarily delay, fine. Permanently cease, never!

The people who use this type of behavior will learn quickly that these inappropriate emotional displays are not effective with you.

Personal Attack

Personal attacks are very similar to the blaming technique in defensive behavior. This manipulation makes you the issue by attacking you personally. The person's delivery style usually intensifies, probably by raising his voice, displaying aggressive nonverbals, and peppering the message with aggressive *you* statements, all intended to establish you as the cause of all the problems. His goal is to take the focus off the attacker and/or to provoke you into an emotional, reactive response.

The acknowledge and refocus technique is effective in this situation as well. "If you would like to discuss my role in this, or my behavior, I will be happy to discuss them with you as soon as we bring this current issue to conclusion."

Another additional assertive diffusing technique is called "two *I*'s and a *we*." "*I* understand that there's a problem and *I* am very anxious to work it out, but *we* will treat each other with respect." This technique clearly establishes your willingness to collaborate, along with your refusal to be attacked or treated disrespectfully.

A third alternative is to identify the personalization and refuse to be manipulated. "I am feeling like this is becoming personal between you and me, but attacking me is not going to make the issue go away. Let's treat each other with respect and focus on the problem."

Perpetual Surrender

This behavior is typical of manipulators, who are quick to give in and resign themselves to perpetual hopelessness. They elect victimization and frequently communicate in phrases such as:

"It's always my fault."
"No matter what I say, it's wrong."
"You're always right no matter what."
"It doesn't do me any good to disagree. What I say isn't
    important."
"Nobody listens to me around here."

These statements are usually followed by withdrawal and a refusal to discuss anything further. Any attempts to resolve issues with these people result in their responding with sighs, blank stares, and passive rehashing of their statements of surrender. (They pout real good too!)

The most effective technique for dealing with perpetual surrenderers is to state, "Obviously, there are some things we need to discuss. I'm very anxious to do so and to hear your side of the story. I'm ready to talk when you are, so let me know when it's a good time to discuss this." Then continue on with business as usual. Do not allow their surrendering to result in your treating them any differently than normal. Especially avoid any sort of pampering or special attention. They want you to leave them alone and pay extra attention to them. Do not allow that to happen.

The Critical Parent

This term is used to describe the people (perhaps your boss) who are predictably and consistently critical of your work. The term captures the spirit of a parent whose child has four A's and one B on her report card. The critical parent quickly pounces on the B! While it may be appropriate to address the B as unacceptable from an extremely brilliant student, it would still be preferable to acknowledge the four A's (80 percent of her work) that were, in fact, perfect. The good work is taken for granted while the problem becomes the focal point for discussion and criticism. You may be in a circumstance where no matter what you do, the good is disregarded and the bad is magnified. As frustrating as these folks can be, there are two strategies that may be helpful.

◆ **On a scale of 1-10.** Ask critical parents this question: "On a scale of 1 to 10, how would you rate this work (project, task, report, etc.)?" Typically they will hesitate and then give it a mid-rating of 5 or 6. This may be an attempt to provoke a negative reaction in you or intentionally hurt your feelings. (Critical parent types are frequently hurtful people—make sure you don't become one; it could hurt your promotability.) Your response, regardless of their rating, is: "Why didn't you rate it *lower?*" The question itself is startling! They expect you to inquire as to why they rated it so low, allowing them to offer negative feedback. By asking them why their rating wasn't lower, you challenge them to identify the positive things they liked. It forces them into a totally different thought process—being complimentary, not critical. Once they identify the positive aspects, the negatives are usually minimal and easily addressed.

   ◆ **Three-two-one.** When critical parents attack, ask them for specific feedback utilizing the following structure."Tell me *three* things you like about this, *two* things you don't, and *one* suggestion on how to do it better." Once again, this approach forces them to acknowledge the positive aspects of your work and denies them the blanket opportunity to be totally critical.

The Complainers

These are the whiners and complainers who perceive themselves to be helpless and hopeless, and who want the rest of the world to share that view. They attempt to gain attention by consistently dwelling on their problems and proclaiming how much worse things really are for them. Complainers reject out of hand any positive input or recommendations for solutions. For example, they will tell you they can't do too much today because they have a headache. If you respond by saying, "I understand how painful that can be, I get bad headaches, too," they see your response as an implied threat. You are obviously trying to shift the subject away from their headache to yours! They quickly escalate the one-upmanship. Their headache will suddenly become the early stages of a brain tumor! (Their problem must be worse than anyone else's.) If you ask them, "What medication are you taking for your headache?", they will tell you that no matter what they take, it upsets their stomach or it just doesn't work. Taking something to correct the problem only makes it worse (poor them). If you were to suggest going to a doctor (sounds like offering a solution!), they will tell you how bad doctors are (doctors can't help—they don't know what they're doing). Complainers dismiss every suggestion because they are striving to receive attention for their problems. They also want their problems to be the basis for lower performance. They should not be expected to meet the standards required of everyone else.

Some effective strategies for dealing with complainers:

1. Be empathetic, never sympathetic

Don't buy into their issues with your sympathy. Empathy is acknowledgment of a problem. Sympathy is feeling sorry for them or creating an emotional connection with their problem. It is appropriate to say, "I understand that headaches can be very painful. I'm sure it's not easy." Do not say, "Oh, I know when I get headaches it takes me hours to get over them." All you have done is given them permission to wallow in their problem for the next couple of hours!

2. Give attention for solutions, not problems

Complainers want attention for their problems. Deny them that payoff. Be responsive to them only when they focus on solutions. Heap attention and recognition on them when they begin to take any initiative to actually solve their problems. They should receive your attention and approval only when they take positive corrective action.

3. Never lower your expectations

The basis for the poor me behavior is rooted in complainers' desire to have you approve or sanction less effort on their part because of their problems. Their identities are not defined by their productivity, but by their problems. They become eternal excuses. Because they think their problems are so unique and intense, they shouldn't be expected to produce as much, perform as well, or to behave as others do. Never lower your expectations. That's what they want. "I know this is difficult for you, but here is what I need you to do . . . (restating the expectations or standards)." Never allow the problems of complainers to lessen their responsibility and accountability.

4. Define your role

Use this communication technique: "Help me understand what you would like me to do. Do you need someone to talk to, just to vent? Or would you like some help with a solution?" Complainers will never admit that they just want to vent. (That sounds bad even to them!) A typical response might be, "Oh, I just want you to know what's going on with me." (They package their information as if it were a public service announcement!) Your response should be, "If you would like some help with this, I'll be happy to take the time. If you need somebody just to listen, I'm happy to do that too, however, I'm extremely busy right now. Let's get together after work." They learn that if they come to you to discuss solutions, you are available and willing to help, but you are not available for venting.

5. Listen to their problems one time

After listening once, if they continue to repeat them, counter by saying, "Is this the same information that we talked about before? Has anything changed since then? Is there anything different? If not, I don't know how to help you and I don't think it is worthwhile for us to spend our time talking about it again. Let's focus on how to either fix it or get over it, but not re-hash the same old problem." Once again, you demonstrate your willingness to help them focus on solutions, and your *un*willingness to just continue wallowing in their problems.

Self-Motivation Assessment

	Yes	No
1. Does my motivation come from within?	☐	☐
2. Do I hold others accountable when I don't feel motivated?	☐	☐

	Yes	No

3. Do I have specific long-term goals that allow me to keep my focus on the future? ☐ ☐

4. Do I believe that I am *as good as it gets,* with no room for improvement? ☐ ☐

5. Do I take the time to celebrate my success, growth, and development as I strive to improve? ☐ ☐

6. Do I interpret the frustrations, problems, and failures of my day-to-day work life as monumental or insurmountable? ☐ ☐

7. Do I see problems and frustrations as challenges to be dealt with, and put behind me? ☐ ☐

8. Do I expect my self-motivation to be assumed or automatic without having to be developed? ☐ ☐

9. Do I have things I do each day to keep myself motivated? ☐ ☐

10. Do I ignore the role that diet, rest, and exercise play in my self-motivation? ☐ ☐

11. Do I effectively and consistently manage my stress? ☐ ☐

12. Do I allow the behaviors of difficult people to de-motivate me? ☐ ☐

13. Do I effectively minimize the impact difficult people have on me? ☐ ☐

14. Do I react negatively or impulsively to difficult people? ☐ ☐

15. Do I handle criticism of my work well? ☐ ☐

16. Am I drawn in to the personal problems of others? ☐ ☐

Scoring:

No responses to the odd-numbered questions and *yes* responses to the even-numbered questions indicate opportunities for improvement.

Pay special attention to questions 1, 2, 12, 13, 14, 15, 16. These address personal responsibility and the control or influence you give to others over your personal self-motivation.

The Four Ps

Here are several strategies for visibly demonstrating your self-motivation.

Work Harder When the Boss Is Not Around

Most people are at their high point of activity and effectiveness when they are under the observation of their bosses or other organizational authorities. It takes no talent to work hard when you are being watched! Your self-motivation shines through when your productivity remains consistent or increases in the absence of supervision. This demonstrates your ability to work in an unsupervised environment and to maintain your own personal internal motivation. This is very impressive indeed.

Document Your Incremental Success, Growth, and Development

As you compete with yourself, raising that bar a few inches at a time, document your success. Identify the most objective measurement possible and utilize this proof at every opportunity, including during performance appraisals, meetings, or monthly reports. Be wary, however, of crossing the line to crass self-promotion.

 If your success is objectively and accurately documented, it is not bragging—it is fact!

When in Doubt, Take Initiative—Become an Agent of Action

Demonstrate your self-motivation by electing to take initiative and shunning inaction whenever possible. If action is called for and no one else is around to initiate it, take it upon yourself to implement it. Communicate your awareness that your actions are outside of the box, or perhaps beyond your scope of authority, rather than risk a lost opportunity or a potential problem due to nonresponse. You choose to take the initiative. Do not consistently overstep your authority or boundaries, and quickly retreat when you do, but seize every opportunity to demonstrate your willingness to take risks and showcase your self-motivation. Be wary that consistent behavior of this type on your part may begin to make your boss insecure, so effective communication is essential. Clarify your motive and thought process *as early as possible*. Position yourself to be seen as a person of action, not inaction, and minimize the threat to your boss.

Demonstrate Your Flexibility

Flexibility is the ability to quickly and effectively embrace change. This is both the emerging change of the moment as well as the long-term monumental and revolutionary change facing every person in every organization. Flexibility is also the willingness to support change even when you are not totally in agreement. Visibly demonstrate your ability to overcome your own personal agendas and skepticisms by supporting the greater good of the organization.

Demonstrate Your Self-Motivation to Others

When you are involved in activities outside of work, be sure that others become aware of your participation. Let them know that you are motivated to improve and grow in every aspect of your life. Obviously, outside activities can be detrimental to your career if they are seen as interfering with your productivity or dedication, however, when in balance, your willingness to pursue achievement in other areas is beneficial to your promotability. If you are involved in exercise programs, service organizations, youth, religious, or other community activities, let people know.

Cultivate your image as a "doer" in all aspects of your life.

Display and Share Your Motivational Resources

Keep your library of motivational resources visible to others. While this can be difficult in today's "cubically-challenged" world where space is at a premium, people are impressed and impacted by what they see displayed in your workspace. As you discover effective motivational resources, books, tapes, interactive programs, and the like, share them with others. When you read a particularly motivating book, buy a copy for someone else. (Don't give yours away. Most people don't return books, tapes, or CDs, which will turn your eagerness to share into a point of contention. You're better off giving them their own). Most of these resources are relatively inexpensive and make great gifts for coworkers. Your thoughtfulness will be appreciated and you will gain a reputation as someone always helping others to improve themselves.

Buy extra copies of this book and share it with your boss and other promotion decision makers. Let them know what great stuff you are reading!

Communicate Work Overload Early

Frequently you will find yourself with an excessive workload, and if not addressed, it can lead to overload and become an overwhelming and de-motivating burden. This becomes visible to others, and while they do not know the source of the de-motivation, they certainly will see the visible signs.

You may be hesitant to speak up about increased work assignments for fear of appearing resistant or unwilling to help. This silence only compounds the problem. It is necessary to communicate your workload needs and establish realistic expectations. Doing so effectively clearly emphasizes your motivation to perform well, and applies your time and effort to the most important priorities. While it is easy to resent your boss for overloading you and piling the work on, it's important to realize that it is your job to communicate your overload. It's not your boss's job to keep track of your current workload. Use this communication technique to clarify your circumstances and reemphasize your motivation to address the tasks that have the highest priority.

1. Acknowledge the importance of the boss's request—"I understand this is important and I'm very anxious to get it done."
2. Summarize your current situation or workload—"I have five tasks that must be completed by the end of today, and I have a quality advisory meeting from 3:00 to 3:30."
3. Clarify prioritization (invite the boss to become your consultant)—"Help me understand which of these things to delay in order to get this new task done." Or, you can offer an alternative solution—"John will probably be able to get this done sooner, or I can complete it for you by tomorrow."

When you communicate the fullness of your workload and your high motivation and willingness in a manner that does not express exasperation, stress, or resentment, you create the opportunity for you and your boss to collaborate on prioritization. You will be applying yourself to the things he deems most important.

Real-World Promotion Mentoring

Frank Condello is the Director of Sales and Marketing for the Nebraska Book Company in Lincoln, Nebraska. Nebraska Book is a multidimensional company serving over 3,000 college and university bookstores throughout the country. They maintain an inventory of approximately three million new and used college textbooks, along with providing information systems and consulting services to their clients.

Frank had these thoughts on visibly demonstrating your self-motivation:

> *Take on some of your bosses' toughest assignments. They have a lot of tough projects they would be willing to give you if you asked—the things they are procrastinating on, don't want to do, or don't have time to do. If you have the skill and the ability, take a chance, even if it doesn't work well. It's your first attempt and they will appreciate whatever you have done. If nothing else, give them a try. Finding people willing to help can be a big problem for anyone who is facing projects. It's really important to help make your bosses look good, and you want to have their blessings as you are promoted.*

When asked about the skills that are critical for future promotability, Frank responded:

> *Of course, in this day and age you must be computer literate. I also think people are looking for individuals who are customer service oriented who would be able to perform in the middle management group, having both the skills of front-line specialists and the skills of managers. The skills to do both—the worker and the manager or the worker and the thinker—will be very important. Being creative and having an economic background is also very critical. As organizations maintain that lean and mean focus, people who understand the process of growth and also the economics of business are very valuable.*

Obviously, Frank believes promotable people are those who possess a broad range of skills and can wear many hats.

In response to a question on determining the realistic organizational opportunity for promotion, Frank had this to say:

> *Look to some of the people who have been with the organization a long time. Sit down and ask them what changes they've*

seen during that period of time and what they think the future holds. Pick their brains and say, "Where have you come from? What were the slowest years in the company? What held it back? What's making it advance now? How do you feel about the future?" Ask the people who are in relatively responsible positions how they feel, and if they were starting out today, just getting into the business, how would they feel about the growth of the company based on what they already know.

In chapter 9 we will examine the realities and techniques concerning performance appraisals that will help you increase your impact, visibility, and promotability. To lead into this discussion, Frank shared these thoughts:

The performance evaluation is in itself an indicator of what the company is looking for as far as your performance. These are the things that are extremely important, either to your supervisor or the organization. Knowing that is a key. Do everything you can to encourage your manager to be extremely candid with you. You can only do a better job if you know the things that you're doing wrong. Rather than get defensive, be prepared for both the good and the bad. Also, as your manager is talking, ask questions. Don't just sit there and listen to the whole thing and stare blankly. Ask, "What do you want me to do?" or "How do you want me to react to this particular situation?" Don't argue the points. Bring certain facts forward that deal with the evaluation that your manager might not be aware of, but it's important to be willing to learn from criticism in the appraisal.

THE PERFORMANCE APPRAISAL PROCESS

The performance appraisal process is probably the most valuable *formal* tool you have at your disposal for enhancing your promotability. Unfortunately, it is a process that is frequently misused, misunderstood, and squandered as an asset to career enhancement.

The performance appraisal process presents the opportunity to:

- ◆ Officially state your objective of obtaining a promotion.
- ◆ Determine the realistic opportunity for achieving the goals you have established.
- ◆ Discover the formal and informal perceptions of your performance and promotability, by your boss and the organization.
- ◆ Objectively present your accomplishments.
- ◆ Evaluate weaknesses and opportunities for growth.
- ◆ Plan the path to improvement and growth.

Ten Real-World Performance Appraisal Realities

To understand and utilize the performance appraisal process to your advantage, there are ten real-world performance appraisal realities that you should consider:

1. The Performance Appraisal Is the Most Effective Mechanism You Have to Determine Your Boss's and the Organization's Perceptions of You

The performance appraisal is your best opportunity to get a clear, concise understanding of how you are perceived. While you may disagree with that perception, its importance and impact cannot be denied. As we have discussed throughout this book, your primary challenge is to change any negative or unflattering perceptions others have about you, and further develop and increase those that are positive.

No one wants to have his performance judged critically or receive negative comments, however, this valuable feedback helps to identify any roadblocks to your promotability. Accept the information and strategically plan to address the challenges. Don't run from them or steep yourself in denial.

2. Most Managers Aren't Trained to Conduct Effective Performance Appraisals

Facilitating a performance appraisal is an untaught skill among American leadership. The truth is, most managers would rather take a beating than conduct performance appraisals. They view them as major hassles and necessary evils to meet company policy requirements. While the performance appraisal is a valuable management tool, an overwhelming majority of managers are not equipped to use it effectively.

Your challenge will be to actually help guide your manager through the process and insure that the results are in your favor. Don't wait for her to ask the right questions. You will have to predetermine the information you want to present and find creative and assertive ways to insure its introduction. You can become the informal stage manager for this production!

3. Performance Appraisals Typically Rate Short-Term Performance Only

Most performance appraisals are intended to judge a one-year period, however, the actual rating time is usually only 90-120 days. The three- or four-month period immediately preceding the appraisal is usually rated, because most appraisals are conducted from *memory* only. Rarely are managers prepared with enough long-term documentation and information to effectively assess the entire twelve-month period. Employees in every organization have learned that the time to kick your performance into gear is about ninety days before your next appraisal. This results in pre-appraisal performance spiking. For the nine months or so after a performance appraisal, productivity is relatively stable, but for the three months immediately preceding the appraisal, the performance increases dramatically.

To enhance your promotability it is important to insure that your performance does not spike just prior to the appraisal, but is consistently high throughout the entire rating period.

4. Most Managers Tend to Be Flowery in Their Appraisal Assessments

Lacking the training to conduct effective performance appraisals, most managers are uncomfortable with presenting critical comment. Not knowing how to do it and anticipating a negative, perhaps volatile reaction from the person being appraised, they avoid candor. Most would rather rate someone inappropriately high than face the hassle of a more accurate lower assessment. It is equivalent to a teacher or school system giving poor or failing students passing grades just to avoid hassles and move them out.

This reluctance to confront weaknesses may result in your not receiving an accurate picture of how you are perceived by your manager or the organization. (This obviously is *not* in your best interest.) As painful as negative feedback may be, it is extremely important that you encourage your appraiser to be open and honest with you. It is critical in developing an effective game plan for future promotion.

5. Most Employees Being Appraised Defend Their Potential Raise by Rejecting Criticism

Because performance appraisals and compensation increases have been directly tied together, it is extremely difficult for many people to acknowledge weaknesses or the validity of critical comment. The reason is very simple. Agreement with a negative assessment may reinforce the decision to offer less money or actually deny any increase in compensation. Typically, when money comes into play, objectivity goes out the window. Most people aggressively defend themselves in an attempt to increase the size of their raise.

It is important for you to change your personal perception of the connection between performance appraisals and compensation. Instead, link the performance appraisal to your promotability. Compensation issues will ultimately be addressed in your favor when you are successfully promoted. Don't defend yourself to protect your money—be open to criticism to improve your long-term prospects.

6. The Performance Appraisal Document Is Typically Ignored Until the Next Appraisal

Most performance appraisals are not living documents, they are filed and ignored until the next performance appraisal period. There is little or no follow-through and the appraisal is not used to measure or improve ongoing performance. This again reflects the fact that most performance appraisals are seen as necessary to comply with policy, and not as valuable instruments for evaluation, growth, and development. It is in your best interest to structure consistent reviews of the appraisal documents to emphasize your performance and identify any achievements during the interim period.

7. Performance Appraisal Priorities Change Frequently, Rendering Agreed-Upon Objectives Obsolete

Goals, priorities, and objectives are negotiated and agreed

upon, but then the appraisal document is filed away to be resurrected only in preparation for the next year's performance appraisal. Typically, by then the previously agreed upon goals, priorities, and objectives are humorous and outdated. The original plans shifted quickly, and probably became outdated and obsolete one week after the appraisal. They were no longer considered important, and you may have spent your last year in pursuit of totally different goals, priorities, and objectives. In most performance appraisals significant time is wasted mutually agreeing that the goals, priorities, and objectives originally set are really no longer appropriate and should be disregarded as the basis for assessment. When this happens, the performance appraisal process tends to shift away from objective measurement and becomes subjective and opinion driven. (This is another reason why many managers are flowery in their assessments, resulting in meaningless evaluations.)

8. Managers Rate Subjectively

This is good news/bad news. If your boss likes you, it's great. If he doesn't, it's a significant roadblock. The greater the subjectivity of the performance appraisal, the more emotion and opinion come into play, and the less influential your actual work performance becomes. In fact, most people who receive low performance appraisals believe that their job performance is really fine, but their manager "just doesn't like them."

 Managers are human beings, and because of their subjective rating tendencies, it is very important to build strong relationships with them.

It is also to your great advantage to have your assessment based on as much objectively measured criteria as possible. Facts and figures speak for themselves and are valuable for neutralizing any possible negative, subjective assessments.

9. Unclear, General, and Unmeasurable Subjective Language Has Become the Norm

The increase of nonspecific language has become very frustrating. People are told they must, *improve, get better, work harder,* or *increase their performance* without any clarification of the meaning or measurement of these terms. How does someone *get better?* What does *better* mean? A typical point of contention in many performance appraisals is an employee's belief of personal improvement, while the manager perceives no change. Neither side has anything but opinion to support these statements (and the boss's opinion wins!). Avoid allowing the encroachment of nonspecific, subjective terms into your performance assessment. As these increase, your control decreases. Ask for specific clarification. Does *getting better* mean a 10 percent increase, a 2 percent decrease, or the total elimination of something?

10. Performance Appraisals Are Typically "One Size Fits All"

The same appraisal format is often used to evaluate every employee regardless of function. It is difficult to present yourself as unique and exceptional when you are grouped as merely one of the crowd by the structure of the process. Your goal is to package yourself as a "custom-built product" in an "off-the-rack world." This is far from easy, but some suggestions follow on how to make this happen.

The Three Stages of the Performance Appraisal

The performance appraisal process has three distinct phases—preparation, presentation, and follow-up. Your grasp of these processes and the ability to perform well in each phase will have a tremendous impact on your promotability.

Preparation

The initial stage is preparation—what you do to prepare for your appraisal. The process is too important to be left to chance.

The better prepared you are for your performance appraisal, the more control you exercise.

Gather Information/Documentation

To prepare effectively for your performance appraisal, you must have copies of all of your previous appraisals, including the most recent. These are necessary to determine your success at meeting the stated objectives, and to establish the upward trends of performance improvement. It is also important to have documentation of your success during the current performance period. This will include:

- ◆ Copies of all reports addressing productivity
- ◆ "Atta boys" or "atta girls" from your boss, internal or external customers, or anyone else who matters!
- ◆ Notes or summaries of meetings or discussions where goals, objectives, or priorities were changed
- ◆ Copies of attendance/absentee records to verify compliance or provide the basis for explanation
- ◆ Formal proof of internal or external achievements (certificates of completion for training/educational programs, certifications obtained, etc.)

Determine Your Objectives

Determine the specific objectives you want to accomplish with your performance appraisal. While these may vary, typically they will be:

- ◆ Identification of your goals and feedback on specific career growth objectives
- ◆ Acknowledgment of your current high level of performance
- ◆ Identification of three opportunities for improvement to enhance promotability

Anticipate Topical Issues

While it's impossible to predict every topic or comment that may be included in the performance appraisal, it is realistic to anticipate the types of issues you think will be addressed. Be prepared with as many facts and data as possible to present your side of the story. Do *not* prepare yourself to aggressively refute every criticism.

> *Critical comment is unpleasant and inevitable. It is valuable to prepare yourself in advance to allow yourself to accept and learn from it.*

Acknowledging your manager's observations and the validity of comments will help the performance appraisal go smoothly. Prepare yourself to be a sponge absorbing information, not a rock repelling it.

Request a Timely Appraisal

Approximately forty-five days prior to your anticipated appraisal date, send a memo to your boss acknowledging the approaching date and asking to establish a specific, mutually convenient time. It is not uncommon for managers to procrastinate scheduling and conducting performance appraisals. You can help overcome this by initiating the contact. Don't wait for your manager to come to you to establish the appraisal date, you go to her to determine the most appropriate time. Any subsequent delays or deviations from the normal pattern should be noted in writing and retained as part of your personal documentation. "At your request, my performance appraisal has been rescheduled for . . . "

Prepare Factual Verification to Support Your Statements

Unverified statements are nothing more than unsubstantiated claims, and lend themselves to subjective debate. This debate can create animosity that may spread to other areas of the performance appraisal. It is better to say nothing than make a statement that you cannot back up with factual data. Carefully assess the value of, and any possible downside to, the statements or issues that you are likely to introduce into the discussion, and ask yourself, "If challenged, could I prove this?".

Practice Your Presentation

Practice what you want to say as well as how you will say it (your tone of voice, your body language, etc.). Practice in a mirror and take care to insure the appraiser sees what you want them to see and not an unaligned visual picture that may distort your message. Also, practice how you will look when you receive critical comment. Your body language, demeanor, and other nonverbal communicators are extremely critical. Practice by tape recording your planned statements and assess your tone of voice. Your performance appraisal is much too important to leave to chance.

 Do not enter your performance appraisal unprepared and expect to create effective and masterful responses on the spur of the moment.

Get a Good Night's Sleep

Be well rested and in a positive frame of mind for your performance appraisal. While it may not be possible, try to schedule the appraisal during your peak energy time of the day. Also, do your best to look good. Dress in your best business attire to give yourself the confidence that will serve you well.

Presentation

The second stage of the process is the actual face-to-face performance appraisal meeting. This critical stage is your opportunity to display your skills, maturity, and total depth of understanding of your role and the organization's goals.

Clear, Concise Delivery

Preparation helps to insure your delivery of information clearly and succinctly. Your performance appraisal has a time limitation (usually sixty to ninety minutes). Don't squander the time with a rambling, disjointed presentation.

Help Your Manager Stay on Track

Knowing that managers often are not trained effectively for the process, there are many subtle techniques you can use to help them stay on track. Most managers will welcome your co-operation and guidance!

Start your performance appraisal by assertively taking control. "I know our time is limited and I am anxious to hear your assessment of my performance and what your expectations are for the coming year. Let me state up front that my goal is to be promoted, and I want to learn the things that I must do to improve my performance for promotability. I am anxious to hear your thoughts. Can we begin?"

There is no guarantee that your manager will allow you to guide the process, and in fact, there may be a very specific format you are required to follow (another example of one-size-fits-all). If you are allowed, consider these key points:

- Always invite your manager to offer his perspective first. This provides you the opportunity to offer any positive affirmation or countering information.
- Separate the assessment of current performance from the establishment of future objectives. They should be two separate and distinct parts of your appraisal.
- The easier you make the appraisal for your boss to conduct, the better impression you will make.

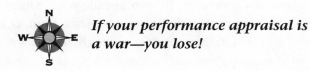

If your performance appraisal is a war—you lose!

Listen Carefully

The greater the stress and pressure, the more selective listening increases. You cannot afford to misinterpret anything that is being said during your performance appraisal. Implement the active listening techniques discussed in chapter 4, especially the restatement of what you have heard. Do *not* wait for the manager to ask you to summarize her message. Assertively take the initiative by saying, "I want to be sure that I am listening accurately. What I heard you say was . . . " It is of paramount importance for your restatement to be unemotional and devoid of any hints of sarcasm, condescension, or provocative inflection.

Mentally Separate the Appraisal from Your Compensation Increase

Of course you want an increase in your compensation, and you may or may not be happy with what is offered. If compensation is discussed during your performance appraisal (which I hope is not the case) and you are not satisfied with the offer, by all means counter with any reasonable request, supported by verifiable fact. You will not get more money because you *deserve* it or because you *need* it. The only reason anyone will increase your compensation is if you have earned it and can prove your increased value. Do not allow money to be the focal point of your performance appraisal. Your goal is to be promoted, which will help solve all of the issues of compensation!

Although difficult to do, separate the money issue in your mind. Increased compensation is short term . . . you have more compelling long-term objectives.

Anticipate and Welcome Criticism

Critical comments offered during a performance appraisal provide a tremendous opportunity to demonstrate your maturity and truly distinguish yourself from the organizational herd. One of the primary reasons managers shudder at the thought of conducting performance appraisals is dealing with the predictable, negative reaction that typically erupts any time they offer critical comment. People become defensive, angry, and frequently display inappropriate emotions at the slightest hint of criticism. Your ability to process it with maturity, and a willingness to improve yourself will set you apart from the crowd. "Thank you for being honest with me. Feedback is a gift and it will help me grow. So many managers are reluctant to be totally candid."

Process Criticism

- Ask for specific examples of the performance or behaviors that are criticized.
- Acknowledge the appropriateness of the perception (this doesn't necessarily mean you agree).
- Identify specific corrections that must be made (not *getting better, improving,* etc.).
- Establish the criteria that will be used to determine correction.

Positive feedback always feels better and affirms your worth, but negative feedback properly received increases your value.

Determine Your Manager's Perception of Priorities

Accomplishing what your manager thinks is important is extremely critical to your promotability, and the best way to do this is by listening to what he wants, and determining the importance he attaches to the various aspects of your job. If your perception of the priorities is different, you may choose to discuss or negotiate them, but in the final analysis, your manager's perception wins.

In your quest for promotion, being the renegade or different drummer is not a highly recommended strategy. Finding out what your boss wants you to accomplish and doing it is!

Seek Specific Input

Along with any additional topics that may be discussed during the performance appraisal, you must determine your manager's opinion of your skills and abilities in the following areas:

- Overall quality of work
- Cost control/budget concerns
- Critical thinking
- Decision making
- Creativity
- Organizational skills
- Communication skills
- Interrelational skills

Failure to determine these views leaves you in the dark. Assume nothing—ask!

Communication Style

The effective use of the assertive communication style discussed in chapter 4 is extremely important in your performance appraisal. Utilize *you* statements only when being complimentary. Avoid any inflammatory comments or using any words or terms that could contain double or hidden meanings. Disagreement is fine, but never allow it to become personal. "I don't agree with that decision" sends a far different message than "That's the dumbest decision I've ever heard."

If either party leaves a performance appraisal saying to themselves, "What did she really mean when she said . . . ?" or "I know what she said but what did she really mean?" then the appraisal has been a colossal failure.

Compliment Your Boss

Communicate to your boss his strengths and the areas where you find him to be particularly helpful. The performance appraisal is an opportunity for two-way recognition and allows you to give your boss very specific examples of the things he does well. There is a thin line between giving positive, upward recognition and being seen as pandering or buttering someone up, however, don't squander the opportunity to give your boss positive feedback. He needs it as much as you do.

Ask for Additional Help, Information, or Support from Your Boss

Along with giving your boss positive comments, you also want to identify areas where she may be of assistance, then request the information that you believe to be helpful. Again, be cognizant of your communication style. Do not say, "You don't give me this information and I really need it." Phrase it alternatively by saying, "Here is the information that I would like to receive. It would be very helpful to me."

Recognize Others

Give appropriate credit to the people who have been helpful to you during this performance appraisal period. Whether it be coworkers, other departments, or specific individuals, let your boss know who it was and what they did. Your willingness to acknowledge the contributions of others in a formal performance appraisal setting reinforces your interpersonal skills and indicates your "big picture" view. You may also wish to encourage your boss to share this information with the specific people you are mentioning. This could be extremely helpful in your quest for promotability.

Identify Conflicts and Remedies

If you are facing specific problems or perhaps conflict situations, it is appropriate to identify them. This is accompanied by your suggestions for correction or requests for your manager's help. Do not use the appraisal opportunity to complain or vent. Also, make sure your comments are not critical of specific individuals. The identification of problems or challenges with individual people is probably best left to more informal discussions. Such topics are not a good use of your limited performance appraisal time.

Follow-up

This third stage of the process addresses what you do after your appraisal and before you begin to plan for the next one.

Your performance appraisal is a valuable tool if you transform it into a living document. To accomplish this, there is an excellent strategy called the *one-three-eight*.

The One-Three-Eight Strategy

The one-three-eight strategy provides for:

◆ One formal performance appraisal
◆ Three quarterly reviews
◆ Eight monthly reporting points

This strategy allows your performance appraisal to be the focus of your activity and provides the constant opportunity to maintain your boss's awareness of your productivity, achievements, and promotability. It also allows you to identify performance problems or changes early on so they will do less long-term damage to your career. This also helps your boss to judge your consistent performance all year long, not just during those pre-appraisal spikes of increased productivity.

◆ **The one.** This indicates your one annual formal performance appraisal. Using the techniques previously discussed, it is extremely important to prepare and present the most effective performance appraisal you can. However, once a year is not enough.

◆ **The three.** Request three formal quarterly reviews of your performance with your boss. Typically, these last a maximum of one hour and are designed to:

Update progress
Identify barriers or roadblocks
Detect early warning signs of potential problems
Negotiate mid-course corrections
Acknowledge shifts in priorities, goals, and objectives

Discover emerging negative performance or behavioral patterns

(You do not want to wait a full year to discover a possible problem. The quicker you discover problems, the sooner you can correct them and the less damage they will do.)

Three quarterly reviews conducted in the third, sixth, and ninth months after your performance appraisal provide multiple interim opportunities for a specific review, update, and analysis of your performance. Your boss will be reluctant to agree to these sessions if they become contentious or drive defensive behaviors on your part. However, if they are assertive, factual assessments of progress, or the lack thereof, and clear lines of communication are established and maintained, your boss will welcome these opportunities for interaction. The success of these three quarterly reviews rests solely on your shoulders.

Create a written summary (one page) of these three meetings, with copies to the boss and your appraisal file.

◆ **The eight.** During the eight remaining months (months one, two, four, five, seven, eight, ten, and eleven from the date of your performance review) create a one-page executive summary for your boss, identifying any current activities relating to your performance appraisal. This should be a very concise report using the following format:

1. Goal/ Objective	Monthly Outcome or Activity	Measurement or Proof Statement	Projections Comments
"Here is the goal."	"This is what I've accomplished."	"This is verification."	"This is what I expect to happen."

2. Offer specific examples of anything that reinforces your promotable abilities or that will impact your promotability. "I am continuing to serve on the cross-functional

quality implementation team," or "I taught Hunter how to use the new software package."

3. The good—"This is going well."
The bad—"This is more challenging than anticipated."
The ugly—"This could be a major problem."

If your boss requires more information on a particular item, he will obviously request it. This monthly summary must be factual and relevant to your performance. Initiate this process on your own, don't wait to be asked, and tell your boss that you are supplying this information to keep him updated and keep the lines of communication open between the two of you.

Together, the twelve documents provide an excellent basis of information for your next performance appraisal and the foundation of an interrelated ongoing process.

When you are interviewing with future promotion decision makers, these documents provide proof of your performance and your organization. They also serve as great confidence builders for you as you take the time to review them in preparation for any interviews or future performance appraisals. These documents are constant affirmations to yourself of how good you truly are and how prepared you are for promotion.

TEN

CAREER KILLERS AND PROMOTION VIRUSES

Twenty Career Killers Guaranteed to Sabotage Your Promotability

While there are many circumstances that can sabotage or derail your career, here is a list of the Big 20!

Policy Abuses

Consistent tardiness and absenteeism stamp a permanent red flag on your personnel file. Be absent or late only when absolutely necessary. Don't abuse the system. If you take all of your sick days in January or use remaining days at the end of the year just because they are available, you damage your credibility and promotability. When you are absent from work, your overall productivity suffers and others who are dependent upon you have their work patterns disrupted.

 By making yourself more visible in your quest for promotability, you become more conspicuous by your absence.

Bringing Personal Problems to Work

Separate your personal problems from your professional life. The problems of life are inevitable, but don't allow your external challenges to become problems for the organization. Confiding in coworkers, taking extended time off to address nonwork issues, extended personal phone conversations, and so on, all inhibit your productivity and the productivity of others around you. The ability to compartmentalize personal problems and not allow them to penetrate into your work life demonstrates high levels of maturity and control. It identifies you as someone who is able to maintain stability even in the face of negative external events. If you need extensive help with personal problems, take advantage of the employee assistance programs or the myriad of other options available. Do not allow your personal problems to follow you into the workplace.

Rejection of Diversity

The higher you ascend on the organizational ladder, the greater your responsibilities become, and the more diverse the community of people who will report to you, depend on you, and interact with you. Rejecting those who don't look like you, act like you, think like you, and talk like you is dumb (and against the law)!

 Presenting yourself as bigoted or in any way intolerant of others' differences will not only prevent promotion, it may cost you your job!

Inappropriate Work Relationships

Develop your personal relationships outside of your workplace. Inappropriate relationships, clandestine affairs, or any intimate fraternization will *always* come back to haunt you. The risk is too great. Of course, you have a right to have relationships with anyone you choose, just remember you can't have it both ways. The company's moral and ethical code and the prevailing definition of acceptable behavior may differ significantly from yours, and in the case of promotion, your code doesn't count!

Predictable, Consistent and Absolute Negativity

When people can write the script before they talk to you and they know the answer is always no or some negative comment, you literally render yourself ineligible for promotion. Your influence wanes as your predictable negativity increases. Others stop asking for your input or they tune out what you are saying merely because of the repetitive message. Can you disagree? Yes! Can you play the devil's advocate? Yes! However, when you come to work consistently dressed in a bright red suit with horns and a tail, carrying a pitchfork, your credibility and influence suffer dramatically.

Spreading Rumor and Gossip

When you are the traceable source of rumor and gossip, or the illusion exists that you are the root of damaging information, your career will be stopped dead in its tracks. You will be viewed as antagonistic, untrustworthy, and a source of underground anti-management information. Being perceived as possessing these traits most likely won't earn you a promotion anytime soon.

Whining/Complaining

Nobody cares! They have their own issues and problems— they don't want to listen to yours!

Losing Your Cool Under Stress or Pressure

Public meltdowns provide actual proof that you can't handle stress and pressure. A picture is worth a thousand words, and all the apologies and explanations in the world will not erase the visual image of your blowing-up or your *losing it*. You are better off going home or calling in sick than providing a display of emotional "un-control," though your enemies and competitors will love it!

Insubordination

Public challenges to authority or refusing to comply with requests or directives from leadership is a ticket to demotion or eventual termination. If you disagree, do it privately with the manager involved. Don't take it to others, and never make it public. If you believe you are being asked to do something unethical, illegal, or so wrong you can't accept it—go get another job!

Defensiveness

Becoming defensive in the face of critical comment or inquiry, labels you as uncooperative and in denial of reality. It also positions you as being unwilling to accept personal responsibility and intent on deflecting accountability to others. Defensiveness is a wall that attempts to defy resolution, correction, and improvement. Your promotability depends upon your ability to dismantle those walls, not erect them.

The Inability to Lose Well

Nobody likes to lose. Not everything will go your way and you won't always get everything you want. Others may be selected for projects or actually outperform you on specific tasks. It is important for you to be able to deal with this and move on. Negative or defensive reactions in such circumstances can be very harmful to your career. Accept them gracefully, learn from the experience, and prepare yourself to do better next time. Be externally gracious and internally committed to reversing such losses in the future.

Taking Credit for the Ideas and Successes of Others

If you usurp credit for the work of others, negative perceptions will spread like wildfire. Animosity, distrust, and much resentment are created, all of which encourage others to seek revenge or some form of payback. The offended party usually does not hesitate to tell everyone who is willing to listen what you have done (rightfully so), and you have created a vengeful enemy with a long memory.

If having taken credit for other's work can be factually verified, it can do permanent career damage and may result in termination.

Failure to Keep Skills Current

Seeking tomorrow's promotion with yesterday's skill level is bound to be an unsuccessful pursuit. Even if you successfully achieve the promotion, unless you upgrade your skills very quickly, your promotion will be short lived. You will probably lose the new job due to poor performance.

Blaming

Becoming the "blamemeister" and always deflecting negative responsibility to others wears thin very quickly. Blaming others does not separate you from responsibility, it magnifies your unwillingness to be held accountable. It also positions you as the eternal victim, never in control but always at the mercy of others. Blamers present themselves as eunuchs.

Rejecting Measurement

Ducking measurement or trying to blur the lines of accountability indicates a lack of confidence and displays an overall fear that measurement may expose shortcomings. Saying "What I do can't be measured" puts you at the subjective mercy of your boss with no way of proving your ability and promotability. It all becomes opinion, and remember, yours doesn't count.

Don't run from measurement, it actually documents your superiority.

The Illusion of Activity *vs.* Productivity

Getting there early, staying late, and always looking busy when the boss is around is important, however, it does not overcome a lack of productivity. Looking busy doesn't get you promoted, being effective does. Don't assume that your boss and other promotion influencers are easily conned. Productivity, not illusions, will always carry the day.

Reluctance to Make Decisions

Being indecisive or constantly seeking permission and approval before taking any initiative demonstrates weakness and a lack of confidence. Delegating up inappropriately or always going to your boss to discover what should be done instead of making your own decisions or taking your own individualized action, magnifies your *follower,* not your *leadership* capabilities.

You are better off occasionally exceeding your authority and being reprimanded than not fully exercising the authority, empowerment, or decision-making responsibilities you already have.

Distorting or Withholding Relevant Information or Data

Withholding information because it may be personally detrimental or because it's not what somebody wants to hear is a short-term strategy with huge, long-term, downside risks. The negative consequences can be monumental. Information that is withheld will always surface eventually, and the later in the process it shows up, the more damaging the outcome tends to be.

If your boss or other promotion influencers believe you are not forthcoming with information, and it becomes their responsibility to ask just the right questions in order for you to tell them the whole story, your lack of promotion is a foregone conclusion.

Visibly Demonstrating Nonproductivity

Wasting time in the direct line of sight of others, especially your manager or any other promotion decision makers, is a sure ticket to remaining in your current position forever.

- ◆ *Do not* stand around visibly engaging in apparent chit-chat with others. (Even if your discussion is about important work-related issues. How does it look to others?)
- ◆ *Do not* park yourself on the telephone engaged in personal conversations in the view of others.
- ◆ *Do not* bring a novel to work with you to read during hours of productivity.
- ◆ *Do not* do your catalog or online shopping during business hours.
- ◆ *Do not* take extended, long, leisurely lunches or abuse break privileges.
- ◆ *Do not* take continuous, extended "smoke breaks." (If every time your boss looks up or needs you and finds you away from your work area, you haven't contributed to positive promotion perceptions.)

Narrowly Defining Your Responsibilities

Failing to reach out and embrace new tasks or not responding to requests because they are outside of your normal duties give the impression that you are self-centered and unwilling to do what's best for the organization. You present yourself as someone concerned only with your own narrow, parochial area of responsibility, and unconcerned with the overall productivity and efficiency of the organization. Demonstrating a narrow focus or limited field of vision truly inhibits your growth.

Global vision—the ability to see the big picture—gets people promoted.

Promotion Viruses

Just as your body and computer systems can be disabled by viruses, careers can also be infected. Listed below are some of the airborne viruses, communicated verbally from your lips to the ears of others, that may do permanent damage to your career. Here are twenty-five statements for you to instantly remove from your workplace vocabulary. These often-heard statements are tickets to oblivion, not promotion.

1. "That's not my job" or "That's not in my job description."
2. "I wasn't hired to do that."
3. "You're not paying me enough to do that."
4. "When you start paying me more, I'll start producing more."
5. "I told you so."
6. "There's no way that will work."
7. "You didn't ask so I didn't tell you."
8. "It's not my fault."
9. "Nobody told me about it."
10. "Everybody else does it, why are you picking on me?"
11. "I deserve it, I'm entitled."
12. "That's not the way we did it where I used to work."
13. "That's not my problem."
14. "We already tried that years ago. It didn't work then, and it won't work now."
15. "I shouldn't have to do that, I've already paid my dues."
16. "If you think that's bad, let me tell you what happened to me. You won't believe it."
17. "I can't do that."
18. "That decision is dumb and whoever made it must be an idiot."
19. "I'm just doing what I was told."
20. "I work harder than anyone else does around here."

21. "Nobody else does anything extra around here, why should I?"
22. "Don't tell anyone I said this, but . . . "
23. "I've been doing it this way all along. Why should I have to change?"
24. "I believe in change. You need to change and your department needs to change, but not me . . . I'm fine, but you need to change."
25. "Nobody cares about me. What I say just doesn't matter."

IN CLOSING

*There are no secrets to success. It is the result
of preparation, hard work, learning from failure.*

—General Colin L. Powell[6]

Pursuing your promotion is a journey. While the destination is clear, the pathway may not always be. The path to promotion is littered with unforeseen circumstances, challenges, pitfalls, and even possible predators. There is a lot of competition out there and the journey, though ultimately rewarding, is certainly not an easy one.

You are dedicated to achieving your goal. If you weren't, you wouldn't have read this book, and obviously would not be reading these final pages. Your dedication and clear goals are initially your greatest asset for achieving your promotion. Following the guidelines and strategies outlined in this book will position you as an attractive candidate for promotion. You have no control over the skill levels of your competitors, you can only control your own, and it's your choice to pursue growth or to remain the same. Developing these skills will also insure your success in meeting all your future challenges. Once you achieve your promotion, you have to perform at that level to stay there! Even in a worst-case scenario, if you develop your skills, maintain an exceptionally high level of productivity, and are ultimately denied promotion—due to lack of opportunity or internal political maneuvering—you still will have increased your inventory of skills and made yourself much more attractive to any future employers. Once developed and perfected, these skills can never be taken from you, and they will serve you well in all areas of your life.

Good luck! Go forth and make it happen!

NOTES

1. Stephen R. Covey, *The 7 Habits of Highly Successful People* (New York: Firestone/Simon & Schuster, 1989), p. 287.
2. Lani Arredondo, *How to Present Like a Pro: Getting People to See Things Your Way* (New York: McGraw Hill,1991), p. 86.
3. Nido R. Qubein, *How to Be a Great Communicator* (Nightengale Court Audio Presentation, 1988).
4. W. Mitchell, *Taking Responsibility for Your Choices* (Boulder, CO: Boulder, CO: Career Track Publication, 1996), Audio Presentation.
5. Martin E.P. Seligman, *Learned Optimism* (New York: Pocket Books, 1990), pp. 40–49.
6. John Cook, *The Book of Positive Quotations* (Minneapolis, MN: Fairview Press,1993), p. 436.

BIBLIOGRAPHY

Albrecht, Karl. *The Only Thing That Matters: Bringing the Power of the Customer into the Center of Your Business.* New York: HarperCollins, 1992.

Arredondo, Lani. *How to Present Like a Pro: Getting People to See Things Your Way.* New York: McGraw Hill, 1991.

Caroselli, Dr. Marlene. *The Language of Leadership.* Amherst, MA: Human Resource Development Press, Inc., 1990.

Cathy, S. Truett. *It's Easier to Succeed than to Fail.* Nashville, TN: Oliver Nelson Books, 1989.

Chambers, Harry E. *The Bad Attitude Survival Guide: Essential Tools for Managers.* Reading, MA: Perseus, 1998.

Chambers, Harry E. and Dr. Robert Craft. *No Fear Management: Rebuilding Trust, Performance and Commitment in the New American Workplace.* Delray Beach, FL: St. Lucie Press, 1998.

Covey, Stephen R. *The 7 Habits of Highly Successful People.* New York: Simon & Schuster, 1989.

Fast, Julius. *Body Language: The Essential Secrets of Non-verbal Communication.* New York: MJF Books, 1970.

Griessman, B. Eugene. *Time Tactics of Very Successful People.* New York: McGraw Hill, 1994.

Mitchell, W. *Taking Responsibility for Your Choices.* Boulder, CO: Career Track Publications, 1996.

Qubein, Nido R. *How to Be a Great Communicator.* New York: John Wiley and Sons, 1997.

Secretan, Lance H.K. *Reclaiming Higher Ground: Creating Organizations That Inspire the Soul.* New York: McGraw Hill, 1997.

Seligman, Martin E.P. *Learned Optimism.* New York: Pocket Books, 1990.

Solomon, Muriel. *Working with Difficult People.* Englewood Cliffs, NJ: Prentice Hall, 1990.

Walton, Mary. *The Deming Management Method.* New York: Perigee Books, 1986.

INDEX